ENDORSEME

Herbie Newell is on the front lines of helping the church care for vulnerable children, every single one of whom is wonderfully made in the image of God. And yes, once we realize that every person bears the image of God Himself, it totally changes the way we live and love the children, women, and men around us, and around the world.

David Platt
Pastor/Teacher, McLean Bible Church, McLean, Virginia
Author, *Radical & Something Needs to Change: A Call to Make Your Life Count in a World of Urgent Need*

Unfortunately, some Christians would consider themselves pro-life and only apply that to the unborn. Herbie challenges this narrow thinking and graciously shows us what it looks like to truly value ALL LIFE. To view all humans as beautiful people made in the image of God with value and purpose.

Jamie Ivey
Host, *The Happy Hour with Jamie Ivey*
Author, *If You Only Knew: My Unlikely, Unavoidable Story of Becoming Free*

No one I know is more of a model for the protection of the vulnerable than Herbie Newell. In this book, this wise leader shows the church how to think and respond wherever human dignity and the image of God are threatened. This book will strengthen your resolve and inform your next steps as you follow Jesus and as you care for those he loves.

Russell Moore
President, The Ethics & Religious Liberty Commission of the Southern Baptist Convention
Author, *The Storm-Tossed Family: How the Cross Reshapes the Home*

Too many times the Church comes across as being more "pro-birth" than "pro-life". It's wonderful to point to scripture and even science to inform someone on where life begins, but we must also be ready to offer options to this same person once they give birth to the child. To be pro abundant life is the true call of every Christian. *Image Bearers* by Herbie Newell offers crucial information for every Christian who makes the claim to truly be pro-life.

Rick Burgess
Co-author, *How to Be a Man: Pursuing Christ-Centered Masculinity*
Co-host, *The Rick and Bubba Show*

There are multiple reasons why the Sanctity of Life is crucial to the well-being of any culture and also an essential element in a Christian world and life view. *Image Bearers,* written by Herbie Newell, is an inspiring, informative, and engaging treatment of the glorious foundation of the Sanctity of Life – God made us on purpose and with purpose; therefore, we have intrinsic significance and dignity as His image bearers.

Harry L. Reeder, III
Pastor/Teacher, Briarwood Presbyterian Church, Birmingham, Alabama
Author, *3D Leadership: De ining, Developing and Deploying Christian Leaders Who Can Change the World*

In a culture that is increasingly experiencing dramatic shifts towards progressive ideology, there may be no more important topic for the church to consider than the implications of what it means for human beings to be image bearers of God. I'm thankful for the work of my friend, Herbie Newell, and for the emphasis he places throughout this book on the value of human life, not only in the womb, but also in the various circumstances and callings for individuals throughout the course of a lifetime. In our volatile culture, where many claim to be pro-life, the church of Jesus Christ has a unique opportunity to authentically carry the pro-life torch in a way that supersedes political debate and leads people into a genuine encounter with God's design for human life and flourishing. Herbie is carrying that torch well, and he is leading us to carry it with him.

Jeff Norris
Lead Teacher and Directional Leader, Perimeter Church, Atlanta, Georgia

Theology determines your biography ... or at least it should! What we believe about God, human beings, salvation, and about hope for this broken of this world, should drive and shape our everyday lives. However, too many believers allow culture or experience or politics or something else to drive their view of these things. Herbie Newell helps us to think about the doctrine of the *Imago Dei* and what the implications for embracing this doctrine looks like. These implications are massive and include more than being "pro-birth" but actually involves being truly pro-life -- pro every human life regardless of age, stage, race or background. If we truly believe in the *Imago Dei*, then our lives should reflect this belief. I pray that this book will help us all live out what we say we believe, for the good of the world and the glory of God

Tony Merida
Pastor, Imago Dei Church, Raleigh, North Carolina
Author, *Ordinary*

Herbie Newell shares the bleak reality that millions of orphans face in our world today and the harsh existence so many people endure because of a culture that has de-valued life. He challenges us to reject the notion that once a child is born, the "pro-life" victory has been won. There is a role each of us can play in creating a culture that respects and values life from conception until death. No one can do everything, but everyone can do something in this quest to honor and protect life throughout all of its stages.

Kevin Ezell
President, North American Mission Board, SBC

Image Bearers is a book every follower of Jesus should read. It will move you to tears. It will also fill you with hope as it shows us how to move forward in the 21st century in service to others. It is good to be pro-birth. It is even better to be pro-life, from conception to natural birth, for all persons who bear the image of God and for whom Christ died and rose again. I pray this book will be widely read and heeded.

Daniel L. Akin
President, Southeastern Baptist Theological Seminary
Author, *Ten Who Changed the World*

We have not only allowed the enemy of God to deceive our hearts regarding the value of life itself, but we have traded our inheritance as children of God, created in His image, for a hollow, empty, twisted lie. That choice has impacted every area of our lives. Herbie Newell reminds us of God's plans and purpose for us, and he challenges us to STAND UP and assume our role as "Image Bearers." We must!

Terry Meeuwsen
Co-host, The 700 Club
Founder, Orphan's Promise

Herbie Newell presents an invitation that's both as compelling and as costly as those offered by Patrick Henry, William Wilberforce, or Desmond Tutu. It is not merely about ideology or voting. It is, at its heart, what the ancient call of true discipleship always has been: a call to defend the lives of others by giving of our own and to salve the world's pain by sharing in it.

Jedd Medefind
President, Christian Alliance for Orphans
Author, *Upended: How Following Jesus Remakes Your Words and World*

The Bible begins with the creation of mankind into God's image and ends with the re-creation of mankind into that same image. And everything in between is about how He has redeemed His creation in Christ Jesus to that end. Herbie Newell understands this story to mean that our entire lives—from conception to eternity—are caught up in bearing the image of our Creator. In *Image Bearers*, he clearly and biblically sounds the alarm for Christ-followers to expand our fight for life to include more than just the elimination of abortion, but also the pursuit and preservation of God's image at every stage of life that's threatened by neglect, abuse, prejudice, injustice, and perversion. Read him and heed him for the glory of God reflected in His image.

Jim Shaddix, Ph.D., D.Min.
W. A. Criswell Professor of Expository Preaching
Senior Fellow, Center for Preaching and Pastoral Leadership
Southeastern Baptist Theological Seminary

Some books challenge, other books inspire you. Very few books change you. Get ready, Herbie Newell has done this with his new book, *Image Bearers*. Our God is pro-life, not just pro-birth. My mind lit up like a July 4th firework display with the insights presented in this book. Do not plan to read this book, plan on being changed by this book.

Scott Dawson
Founder and CEO, Scott Dawson Evangelistic Association
Author, *Dear Lord Why: Finding Answers to Life's Most Challenging Questions?*

Christ's church stands at the intersection of grace and truth in an increasingly polarized landscape. *Image Bearers* helps its reader to navigate such murky ethical waters in the American church. I appreciate Herbie's willingness to address issues at the heart of ongoing culture wars with the timeless wisdom of God's word. There is no quarter to be held for those holding to a self-centered Christianity marked more by proximity to party lines instead of one's neighbor. Herbie challenges the reader to consistent and faithful biblical witness; measured in effectiveness through the lens of the person and work of Jesus Christ. In *Image Bearers* no one's toes are safe.

Jason Cook
Germantown Outpost Pastor, Fellowship Memphis

In a world beset by violence and corruption, Christians are grasping for a framework by which to engage the world. I believe the Bible's view of *Imago Dei* is the theology we need to desperately recover in order to fulfill both the Great Commandment and the Great Commission. That's why I believe Image-Bearers is an important book for every believer who desires to follow Jesus into the world. This book will help you develop and apply a holistic view of human dignity and motivate you to care for the most vulnerable in our society, written not by academic theorists, but as someone who embodies this ethic every day.

Daniel Darling
Vice President for Communications, The Ethics and Religious Liberty Commission of the Southern Baptist Convention
Author, *The Dignity Revolution*

Image Bearers by Herbie Newell is a vital tool in equipping the saints to the work of ministry through the opportunity of orphan care.

David Nasser
Author and Pastor

As image bearers of our Sovereign creator, we know that we are to preserve, protect and defend life, because all life is sacred... but we have listened to the cultural lies and have become complacent. Herbie re-states our solid footing, eternal mandate, and inspires us to re-engage in the vital, Gospel centered fight for the sanctity of all life. This book is a clarion call to see truth, repent personally and passionately advocate for every individual made in the image of our Gracious God. This is a blessed book, much needed in our churches and communities today.

Andy Lehman
Vice President, Lifesong for Orphans

Herbie Newell has captured God's heart on how we should care for all people. The world would be a better place and the church a stronger force for good if they learned to apply the principles outlined in *Image Bearers*. I hope you will care enough about yourself and others to read this timely resource.

Dr. Scott Reynolds
Pastor, North River Church, Tuscaloosa, Alabama

IMAGE BEARERS

shifting from pro-birth to pro-life

Herbie Newell

Image Bearers: Shifting from Pro-Birth to Pro-Life

Lifeline Children's Services, Inc.
100 Missionary Ridge
Birmingham, AL 35242
LifelineChild.org

Unless otherwise indicated, all Scripture quotations are from
The Holy Bible, English Standard Version.

Editors: Ashley Newell, Rick Morton
Copy Editor: Neisha Roberts
Cover Design: Charity Betts

CONTENTS

DEDICATION

To my beloved Ashley...
*It is because of your God given passion for life and
the unborn that the Lord called us into this work.
I could never do this without you.*

ACKNOWLEDGEMENTS

It is only by God's grace and the help of many dear friends that this book has been completed. It was a labor of love and effort by so many people.

Much of this book has been written abroad in Colombia as well as in India and Poland. To that end I want to give special thanks to the Juan Valdez and Masa coffee shops in Zona G in Bogota, Colombia as well as all of the Delta Airlines first class upgrades.

I am grateful as well for the work and ministry of Lifeline Children's Services and the team of people who have been assembled. They are the heroes of so many of these stories and are on the frontlines. The Lord has been so gracious to surround me with such friends, leaders, and precious followers of Christ.

I want to also thank the National Board of Directors for Lifeline Children's Services. They have extended so much grace to me over the past 16 years by caring well for my family, sharpening my passionate ideas, directing with grace my efforts to lead the ministry, as well as giving me the space to write this book. Thank you all for believing that Christ in me could lead the ministry of Lifeline at such a crucial time as was faced in 2003.

I am so thankful as well to Charity Betts who volunteered her time and talent to typeset, layout, and graphically design this book from the cover, back and every page in between. Your labor of love is such a gift.

I am also abundantly grateful to Neisha Roberts for her edits of the manuscript several times working outside of her job description to use her talents. Thank you to Anna Dickson who willingly edited, corrected, uploaded, and did whatever was needed. Also, I am so blessed to have Sarah Kate Stallings pick up projects so that I could write and edit. She also did whatever was necessary to get this book finished, literally whatever was needed.

This project would never have been started without the encouragement of my dear brother and friend, Dr. Rick (Morton). Not only did he encourage me to write, he encouraged me along the way. He read every chapter countless times giving great critique, encouragement, and abundant help. I love Dr. Rick and am so grateful that the Lord has brought this man of God into my life for so many reasons, and this book is only a small part. So thankful for his precious wife Denise as well, who gave the manuscript one last look for any copy edits and mistakes that we might have missed.

I am indebted to my beautifully precious wife Ashley. The last 18 years of marriage to you have been such a sweet time of partnership for the Gospel. This book was a true project for you as you read it multiple times, completed my thoughts, edited it with care, and took care of life at home so that I could write. You helped in so many countless ways with this project, all the while continuing to run our home, homeschool our three children, and struggling with health issues, "the thorn in your flesh."

And of course, I am abundantly thankful to my family, Ashley, Caleb, Adelynn and Emily. I love you all more than words could ever be expected to express. The four of you are gifts of the Father and I am grateful for the way I see the image of God expressed in each on of you so uniquely. I see the warmth of Christ in Ashley, the empathy of Christ in Caleb, the loyalty of Christ in Adelynn, and the abundance of life of Christ in Emily. I see Him in each of you in so many different ways as well.

Lastly, I want to thank my Lord and Savior Jesus Christ. You have redeemed me, loved me, and daily lavish your grace upon me. Thank you for your Word, and may my life, the ministry that I serve, and the family that I lead reflect your glory every day.

PREFACE

Just about two years ago, God delivered into my life one of the greatest joys I could imagine, our precious granddaughter Mia. For years, I heard over and over from friends a little farther along in the journey than me about the great blessing of grandparenting. Honestly, I thought those friends were overselling it. After all, parenting is pretty great. They weren't exaggerating. Being a parent is a high privilege for sure, but being a grandparent is amazing and fulfilling in completely different ways, especially as we get to experience the blessing of our daughter being a parent.

One of the most fun things about being Mia's "Doc" is having a front row seat to watch Nastia be a momma to a little girl who is her "spitting image." Mia really seems like a two-year-old copy of her momma. She is Nastia's "Mini-Me." The resemblance is striking. Everyone sees it even at a quick glance, but those of us who are closer are really able to see just how much she is working to copy her momma. Getting a front row seat to watching this messy, moody, not-yet-capable little girl imitate her momma has given me a fresh reminder of how much we all have as people created in the image of God. After all, we were created to be God's Mini-Me. Not a clone or an equal, but rather a little representation of the much grander One.

You see, being the image bearers of God is all-defining for us. Though frail and imperfect, the God of the universe created each of us to be a reflection of Him. He fashioned every single person to put Himself on display and to lead us to know Him more fully and to worship Him more intently. Yet in our selfish, busy world, we are all too often blind to the reflection of God in each other.

That's why this book is important. As image bearers of God, we need reminders. We need encouragements. We need admonishments, and that's exactly what I believe you have in your hands in *Image Bearers*.

As those created in the image of God, we stand in need of God's help to fulfill our created purpose of reflecting Him and bringing praise to Him. We are in need of the transforming work of Jesus and the sanctifying activity of the Spirit to conform us to think and talk and act like our Heavenly Father. In the subsequent pages, you will find challenge and counsel from my brother, Herbie Newell, in just what it means to bear the image of God. You will find practical insights into how bearing the image of God calls us to live as completely and wholly pro-life as an act of worship to our Creator. You will find the wise words of a dear brother who practices what he preaches in loving and seeking justice for the vulnerable and the outcast. Most of all, I believe that you will catch a greater glimpse of the God in whose image we are all created and in the work of redemption of Jesus our Lord.

Rick Morton
Vice President of Engagement
Lifeline Children's Services

INTRODUCTION

The 41st President of the United States of America, George H.W. Bush was a pilot in the U.S. Navy before his illustrious public service career that catapulted him to the White House. In 1944, President Bush was Ensign Bush, one of nine relatively unknown naval aviators who survived a crash following a successful raid by the U.S. on an important Japanese broadcasting station at Chichijima.

The President, however, was the only one of the surviving airmen who was able to avoid captivity by the Japanese. The other eight were executed after being brutally tortured at the hands of their Japanese captors. The treatment of President Bush's fellow airmen is not isolated. The brutality of the Japanese during World War II both in their tactics of engagement as well as their treatment of POW's is well documented. For example, Laura Hillenbrand writes in her book *Unbroken* of the torture both witnessed and experienced by Louis Zamperini during his time of captivity by the Japanese.

Japan was a nation dedicated to the worship of their earthly king. The Japanese people were led to believe that only the life of their emperor was sacred, and all other life was expendable. As a result, men led suicide missions with great accuracy and passion. Even in losing battles, the Japanese would inflict much damage because they would rarely retreat. Instead, the Japanese preferred to sacrifice their men in the hopes of weakening their enemy because the lives of individual Japanese soldiers were deemed of little value in light of the value of their emperor.

In stark contrast, the U.S. Navy operated under much different convictions. The Navy sent vessels into the dangerous waters off Chichijima in hopes of rescuing the downed airmen. By the sovereign hand of God, Ensign Bush was found by a U.S. submarine that was sent into harm's way with the hope of rescuing any or all of the survivors. Bush was bobbing on a life raft in the Pacific Ocean unable to help himself. He was delirious, clinging to life, heavily dehydrated, with barely the presence of mind to paddle away from the island to await rescue.

There was a film crew aboard the submarine documenting the rescue which was one of literally hundreds that occurred in the Pacific Theater during World War II. As the world saw from the film crew's efforts, a relatively unknown 20-year-old aviator was rescued. Even the Japanese on Chichijima took note. In fact, one Japanese official, who witnessed the rescue, came to realize later that the U.S. had sent a submarine into danger in order to save just one aviator. This official noted that the Americans had a much different view of life and the value of a single life. He said, "There is no way that the Japanese Navy would have sent any vessel into harm's way, simply for a single aviator. They would have written them off."

The U.S. attitude toward rescuing servicemen differed from the Japanese because of the pervasive belief that all people are created equal, and each person is endowed by the Creator with certain unalienable rights including life, liberty, and the pursuit of happiness.

Of course, this view, penned by Thomas Jefferson in the Declaration of Independence and shared by the founders, came from a distinctively Judeo-Christian view of the sanctity of human life. From the beginning, the U.S. was founded on the belief that life is made by God, sustained by God, and precious to our great God.

Today, we find that we are still in a battle for the sanctity of human life and this battle is not limited to the courtroom or even Capitol Hill. This battle is not only around abortion clinics and in the hearts of women in unplanned and inconvenient pregnancies. This battle is raging in the souls of all people.

In the same way, being pro-life is not merely confined to rhetoric or legal action. It is displaying the love of Christ to the orphan, the single mom, the family who has lost their children to the foster care system, and all image bearers made in beautiful diversity by our God. Being pro-life means that you understand that all life is sacred and valuable. Being pro-life is recognizing that life is formed and fashioned in the womb by a loving Creator who knits us together, forms us like a potter, and fashions us into His image. Life is beautiful and uniquely diverse, and reflects the God who fashioned it.

Being pro-life means that not only do we see abortion as murder, but we also see our apathy against injustice toward life outside of the womb as a co-conspirator in the fight for life. It means we fight for racial equality. It means we love the women on the way into the abortion clinic passionately with the love of Christ, and it means we embrace life no matter what syndrome may be attached to a person's identity.

Being pro-life means that not only do we see abortion as murder, but we also see our apathy against injustice toward life outside of the womb as a co-conspirator in the fight for life.

There are many books written about being pro-life and combatting abortion, but my hope is this small volume will bring awareness that the pro-life ethic is so much bigger than just being pro-birth. As Christians, we are called to understand the *Imago Dei* (image of God). We are made by God, crafted in His Image, and responsible to show His character to a lost and dying world.

As image bearers of Almighty God, my hope is that these chapters will encourage you to be consistently pro-life by looking briefly at several key issues: abortion, caring for those with special needs, racial reconciliation, honoring women, encouraging dads toward presence, rallying godly men, slavery, trafficking, pornography, and adoption and orphan care. In the end, all of these issues come back to a common root: we are called to gospel-driven justice because we are called to be defenders of the *Imago Dei*.

Chapter One
THE CASE FOR LIFE

*Then God said, "Let us make man in our image, after our likeness. And let
them have dominion over the fish of the sea and over the birds of the heavens
and over the livestock and over all the earth and over every creeping thing
that creeps on the earth." So God created man in His own image, in the image
of God He created him; male and female He created them. And God blessed
them. And God said to them, "Be fruitful and multiply and fill the earth and
subdue it, and have dominion over the fish of the sea and over the birds of the
heavens and over every living thing that moves on the earth." ... And God saw
everything that He had made, and behold, it was very good. And there was
evening and there was morning, the sixth day.*

—Genesis 1:26-28, 31

After all creation was spoken into existence, God was not finished. While
creation was perfectly good, wonderfully beautiful, and exceedingly awe-
inspiring, it was not complete. Days one through five of God's creative work
brought distinct and purposeful order. For instance, vegetation was not
created until the mechanisms had been created to sustain them — light, soil,
and water. Animals did not begin to roam until they had the vegetation to
sustain them. God's world was orderly, purposeful, and grand.

Mankind – The Image Bearers

Before man was made, spellbinding canyons existed to be explored. Mountains, like the Himalayas and the Rockies, beckoned to be climbed by something more than a billy-goat or elk. Rivers, streams, and lakes littered all of creation waiting to be forged. God's creation was enjoyable, pleasurable, and "good." Still, something was missing. Creation needed a caretaker, an explorer, and a worshipper. What the Creator wanted was someone who would enjoy the goodness of creation along with Him. He needed an image bearer.

The imprint of God's nature, image, and likeness was placed upon man. While all of creation echoed the praise and pointed to our Great God, only man would be the representative of God. Man was the crown of creation, set in place to do the work of God by naming the animals, tilling the soil, and tending to creation. Man was also set in place to lead creation into the exaltation of her Creator. Man was the leader of worship who was to point, continually, all of creation back to God.

Attack on God's Creation

Man had incredible freedom, important responsibility, and inordinate adventure, but it wasn't enough. In Genesis 3, Satan, the great deceiver, breathed a lie into the hearts of men by twisting the truth of the *Imago Dei*. Man was made in the image of God, but not given the sovereign responsibility of God, and that was a good thing. Satan, as he so often does, tricked man into trading an infinitely "good" thing for temporary satisfaction that ultimately led to shackles. So with the temptation of man, came the first attack on the *Imago Dei*.

> *Man had incredible freedom, important responsibility, and inordinate adventure, but it wasn't enough.*
>
> *In Genesis 3, Satan, the great deceiver, breathed a lie into the hearts of men by twisting the truth of the Imago Dei.*

Paul David Tripp writes in his *New Morning Mercies* devotional,

> *It's important to realize that you can search for life in only two places. Either you have found life to the fullest vertically or you are shopping for it horizontally. This is a major piece of what Paul is writing about in Romans 1:25 when he says: "They exchanged the truth about God for a lie and worshipped and served the creature rather than the Creator, who is blessed forever! Amen." What is that lie? It is the lie that was first told in the garden of Eden— the false promise that life, heart-satisfying life, could be found somewhere outside the Creator. It is the lie of lies, the cruelest lie ever told. If you believe it, it will not only leave you empty and discouraged, but it will set your life on a course of destruction.*

As sin infiltrated the world, even things as simple as our diet were affected. Flesh began to be consumed for sustenance instead of the vegetation that God originally gave for food. Greater changes happened as well. Bloodlust filled the hearts of man, and creation began to war against itself. While it may be hard for many of us to understand vegetarianism today, in the beginning in the Garden, all animals and the people were herbivores, and people did not kill animals for food. The lion was lying down with the lamb, the infant could play in the adder's den without worrying about being hurt, and no animal was labeled as prey.

In the beginning, plants were given as the sufficient source of nourishment to sustain life. Genesis 1:30 tells us, *"And to every beast of the earth and to every bird of the heavens and to everything that creeps on the earth, everything that has the breath of life, I have given every green plant for food."* Furthermore, God told man in Genesis 2:16, *"And the Lord God commanded the man, saying, 'You may surely eat of every tree of the garden.'"* It did not remain that way because sin always births more sin which in turn always brings death and destruction.

Eventually things were so out of control because of the wickedness of man that God brought about the wages of sin immediately to all but Noah and his family.

> The Lord saw that the wickedness of man was great in the earth, and that every intention of the thoughts of his heart was only evil continually. And the Lord regretted that He had made man on the earth, and it grieved Him to His heart. So the Lord said, "I will blot out man whom I have created from the face of the land, man and animals and creeping things and birds of the heavens, for I am sorry that I have made them." —**Genesis 6:5-7**

The far reaching effects of sin found their way even into diets. After the flood and the destruction of all things, God changed the foods people were permitted to eat. God allowed the consumption of meat.

> The fear of you and the dread of you shall be upon every beast of the earth and upon every bird of the heavens, upon everything that creeps on the ground and all the fish of the sea. Into your hand they are delivered. Every moving thing that lives shall be food for you. And as I gave you the green plants, I give you everything. —**Genesis 9:2-3**

There was great purpose even in God's dietary allowances as God revealed Himself to people. While man now had a varied selection of food from which to choose, there were very specific restrictions. These restrictions were very important because they were a reminder of the sanctity of life. God was allowing man to kill animals for food, but in the restrictions, He was reminding them that life still remained sacred. The Lord instructed in Genesis 9:4-6,

> But you shall not eat flesh with its life, that is, its blood. And for your lifeblood I will require a reckoning: from every beast I will require it and from man. From his fellow man I will require a reckoning for the life of man. Whoever sheds the blood of man, by man shall his blood be shed, for God made man in His own image.

Sanctity of Life and the Gospel

From the beginning, the case for life was made. Man possessed the *Imago Dei*. As an image bearer, man was to preserve, protect, and defend life because life is sacred. The whole biblical narrative in fact, is a case for the sanctity of life. Even though all men fell and still fall short of the glory of God, God pursued and still pursues our hearts and our lives.

The greatest evidence of the sanctity of life found in the Bible is that God sent forth His Son, born of a woman and made in the image of God, to live, suffer, and die so that through His resurrection, He might redeem broken image bearers back to God. Beloved, life itself is sacred because we have a Father who paid the ultimate price to sanctify it.

Lest we forget, on this side of the cross and resurrection that the same enemy of Genesis 3, Satan, is alive and well, deceiving men, twisting God's truth, and tempting men's hearts. Satan is our active enemy who *"prowls around like a roaring lion, seeking someone to devour."* We must resist the Devil with every fiber of our being and every resource from the Spirit so that he will flee from us (James 4:7).

Looking ahead, most of the issues addressed in the rest of this book exist because, as a Church and as a people, believers have not resisted the Devil and clung to Christ. Rather, as believers, we have allowed the enemy's deception to woo us into complacency. We've allowed him to deceive our hearts and to frustrate our souls all while ignoring the great truth of the *Imago Dei* and the God ordained sanctity of life.

As the Church of the Lord Jesus Christ, we have been given the mission to reclaim the broken in the name of our Savior. This mission we have received is costly and dangerous. We will raise questions and make truth claims that sinful men do not want to hear. Nevertheless, we must persevere.

Herod – An Example

In his gospel, Matthew reports about Herod the Tetrarch ignoring the sovereignty of God. Herod worshipped himself and clamored for others to worship him as well. Herod saw John the Baptist as a great threat to his worldview and way of living, but he recognized Jesus as a much more ultimate threat.

> At that time Herod the tetrarch heard about the fame of Jesus, and he said to his servants, "This is John the Baptist. He has been raised from the dead; that is why these miraculous powers are at work in him." For Herod had seized John and bound him and put him in prison for the sake of Herodias, his brother Philip's wife, because John had been saying to him, "It is not lawful for you to have her." And though he wanted to put him to death, he feared the people, because they held him to be a prophet. But when Herod's birthday came, the daughter of Herodias danced before the company and pleased Herod, so that he promised with an oath to give her whatever she might ask. Prompted by her mother, she said, "Give me the head of John the Baptist here on a platter." And the king was sorry, but because of his oaths and his guests he commanded it to be given. He sent and had John beheaded in the prison, and his head was brought on a platter and given to the girl, and she brought it to her mother. And his disciples came and took the body and buried it, and they went and told Jesus. —**Matthew 14:1-12**

Frankly, Herod might have been a king, but in the end, he was a man who was like us, easily deceived by the Devil. The Devil appealed to the strong appetites of Herod. John the Baptist stood in the way of Herod's desires being met. Herod hated John because John spoke the truth without fear, but he preserved John because Herod loved his own reputation above all else.

Really, Herod valued no life but his own, and he worked to bolster his own reputation and extend his rule above all others. John the Baptist dared raise questions about the legitimacy of worshipping Herod. John's reasoning offended Herod because it was convicting, personal, and ultimately because the Truth was on John's side. John's questions were not asked out of spite or to cause strife. They were asked to proclaim the gospel and to announce the coming Kingdom of God.

Matthew tells us that Herod hosted a birthday party for himself. In first century Jewish culture, hosting one's own birthday party would have been most audacious. In fact, the custom of the day didn't even allow for celebrating the birth of a living man, because It was only thought proper to celebrate a man's birth once he had died. During his narcissistic birthday party, Herod was so intoxicated and full of his own lustful desires that he made an outlandish oath in order to feed his growing fleshly desire.

The oath brings the death of John the Baptist in a gruesome way. Scenes like these that remind us that the Bible is not a sanitized fairy tale full of PG stories. This shocking account emphasizes that Herod placed his own desire and personal preference above the life of another.

Beloved, this is the same battle we see over the war for the sanctity of life in our culture and time. While it may be easy for us to identify that battle raging in the world around us, the truth is that it is much harder for us to see the same battle alive in our own hearts and consciences. We can tend to be easily deceived as to our own blind spots, and the Devil looks to feed our personal desires so that we become inattentive to God, His precepts, and His mission.

The Devil has only two powers over humankind — the power of deception and the power of accusation. The Devil twists the truth to deceive us and then gives the truth of our condemnation back to us in the most ruthless way possible. No one is more pro-choice on the way into an abortion clinic than the Devil and no one more pro-life as he convicts you on the way out. He is deceiving us and deceiving our neighbor. Then once we have acted upon our deception, he brings the hammer of crippling accusation to remind us of our sin and to render us powerless.

We do not like the message of who we are in our sin. The gospel defines our sin very explicitly. The gospel does not excuse our sin or make it acceptable.

The gospel tells us plainly that our lives and our sin are an affront to a holy and perfect God that can only be slayed by Jesus.

The difference between the gospel of the Lord Jesus Christ and the Devil's accusation is that the gospel addresses our sin and then begins to cleanse our conscience through the mercy of God. Wayward sinner, you can never run too far away from God's great mercy. Our God is merciful, patient, and kind because He made us, formed us, breathed life into us, and calls our life "sacred." Beloved, the only way to defeat the power of the Devil is through the bloody cross and empty grave.

For those who have experienced or encouraged abortion and crave forgiveness, may the words of Psalm 103:8-12 wash over your heart and soul,

> The LORD is merciful and gracious, slow to anger and abounding in steadfast love. He will not always chide, nor will he keep his anger forever. He does not deal with us according to our sins, nor repay us according to our iniquities. For as high as the heavens are above the earth, so great is his steadfast love toward those who fear him; as far as the east is from the west, so far does he remove our transgressions from us.

Paul tells the church at Corinth in 2 Corinthians 5:20-21,

> Therefore, we are ambassadors for Christ, God making His appeal through us. We implore you on behalf of Christ, be reconciled to God. For our sake He made Him to be sin who knew no sin, so that in Him we might become the righteousness of God.

This ambassadorship is why we protect life from the moment of conception in the womb until the sovereignly appointed moment of death that rests in the hands of the Creator. This is why we plead for the fatherless, show dignity to the broken, cherish those with special needs, work toward racial reconciliation, and fight for the gospel to be made known to every tribe, tongue, and nation. Moreover, we who are in Christ are now called out as ministers of reconciliation — working to reconcile the rightful place of the *Imago Dei*.

Beloved, the fight for the sanctity of life is a gospel issue not merely a social issue, and we must expect the fight to be difficult. We must always remember that this gospel mission is dangerous, controversial, radical, and oh so very crucial, but our power to press on comes from our King.

Discussion Questions

1. At the beginning of Genesis God said everything was "good," but He still created man. What does that tell us about His love for life?

2. How have you resisted the Devil and clung to Christ in the case for life? How have you fallen short or been complacent?

3. "No one is more pro-choice on the way into an abortion clinic than the Devil and no one more pro-life as he convicts you on the way out." How does this quote help you understand the Devil's tactics to control this issue? How does viewing this as a spiritual issue help stir up compassion for the lives involved?

4. Whether you have encouraged abortion, participated in abortion, or been complacent about abortion, how does the Gospel and Psalm 103:8-12 shed light on God's graciousness toward all of us?

5. 2 Corinthians 5:20-21 refers to us as "ambassadors for Christ." As a Christ follower, how does that reality sit with you? What responsibilities and privileges of this role come to mind?

Chapter Two

ABORTION

For You formed my inward parts; You knitted me together in my mother's womb.
I praise You, for I am fearfully and wonderfully made. Wonderful are Your works;
my soul knows it very well. My frame was not hidden from You, when I was being
made in secret, intricately woven in the depths of the earth. Your eyes saw my
unformed substance; in your book were written, every one of them, the days
that were formed for me, when as yet there was none of them.
How precious to me are Your thoughts, O God! How vast is the sum of them!

— Psalm 139:13-17

If December 7, 1941, when the Japanese bombed Pearl Harbor was the day of infamy, most American Christians would mark January 22, 1973, as the second day of infamy in U.S. history. This was the day that the term "pro-life" was coined to coalesce with "pro-choice." The legalization of abortion in America was a turning point.

On January 22, 1973, the Warren E. Burger-led U.S. Supreme Court legalized abortion by a 7-2 vote, thus disallowing most state and federal restrictions on abortion in the United States. With this landmark decision, battle lines were drawn from the Supreme Court into the hearts and minds of the American public for the sanctity of life in the womb.

In 1973, the Supreme Court decision of *Roe v. Wade* ruled that state laws banning abortion were unconstitutional. The court ruled that a woman's right to privacy was legally more important than the interest of any state in the protection of an unborn child. The decision ruled that unborn children were not "persons" who were entitled to any protections under our Constitution. With the stroke of a pen, laws banning abortion were nullified and unborn children lost all legal protection. Over one million legal abortions have been performed in the U.S. every year since 1973.

When a society begins to deny life to the most vulnerable and to mark those lives as a "choice," the decline of the society and its value of life will soon follow. Beloved, this is exactly what has happened in America. Today, Darwin's discredited theory of evolution is considered settled fact in the minds of Americans and most of the rest of the world with survival of the fittest being the standard for life and death. In the years since the legalization of abortion, life has become ranked by value, worth, dignity, and health. While what the enemy found in the garden in Genesis 3 has been at war with the *Imago Dei* since creation, for the U.S., the watershed moment was January 22, 1973.

While life certainly had been devalued in other significant ways in the U.S. through slavery and other atrocities, on this day, it became legal and approved to kill life in the womb simply because of convenience. Proponents of abortion rights have made abortion a woman's right and have labeled any who speak against abortion as "anti-woman;" however, champions of abortion rights are woefully inconsistent when it comes to matters of life. They would decry a woman guilty of abuse and murder if she were to harm purposely or kill a one-month old baby while vehemently protecting a woman's right to kill a pre-born child. At its core, the issue of abortion is inextricably tied to our understanding of the *Imago Dei*. When does life become valuable? Is it when oxygen enters the lungs or when the heartbeat starts, or does life begin at the moment of conception?

A simple illustration makes the point. When does a work of art begin? Is it the moment of inspiration when the artist first sets out to create or only once the art is finished? Artisans the world over would argue that a masterpiece begins at the moment of inspirations or, at the very least, when the chisel first hits the stone or the paint first hits the canvas. Art museums in Western Europe including the Louvre in Paris and the Uffizi in Florence, Italy, contain recognized masterpieces that are unfinished pieces of art. Sculptures that Michelangelo never quite finished like the famous *Pietà* or paintings da Vinci gave up on like the *Adoration of The Magi* are regarded as some of the world's greatest pieces of art yet they were never completed by their creator. If we celebrate these unfinished works of art as masterpieces, why do we devalue something far greater — the Master Creator's work of life?

The Tragedy of Abortion

September 11, 2001, was a clear, sunny Tuesday in New York City. The Major League Baseball season was nearing an end, and the Yankees were once again in first place with the Chicago White Sox in town. Men and women scrambled from all across the many boroughs of New York City, dropping kids off at school and jumping into the frantic pace of a city that never sleeps and never stops working. It was just a normal Tuesday in Manhattan until 8:46 A.M. Eastern Daylight Time.

Al Qaeda terrorists coordinated the hijacking of four passenger airplanes and successfully carried out three planned suicide attacks against the World Trade Center in New York City and the Pentagon in Washington, D.C. Terrorists killed everyone on board the planes and nearly 3,000 people on the ground. The fourth plane was apprehended by passengers who were able to crash into a Pennsylvania field, killing all on board, but sparing any greater carnage on other targets.

These attacks, which changed the course of the nation and President George W. Bush's presidency, were the largest attacks by any foreign power on American soil and still remain the deadliest day in American history not associated with a major world war or conflict. Not only was the loss of life abundant, but also damage to American infrastructure was vast. Much of the World Trade Center had collapsed including the skyline landmarks of Tower 1 and Tower 2, at the time the worlds' tallest buildings. Additionally, a gigantic gaping hole was left in the Pentagon. September 11, 2001, would forever be etched into American history as 9/11.

Once most of the rubble had been removed at the World Trade Center site, a memorial was quickly erected to remember all of those who had lost their lives as a result of the attack, including those first responders who heroically rushed into the towers to save people trapped by the fire and smoke. The first true memorial for 9/11 was two huge spotlights, which illuminated the space where the two iconic towers had once proudly stood. The mantra of the aftermath of 9/11 was, "We Will Never Forget."

Fast-forward nearly 18 years to January 22, 2019. Many years after the World Trade Center complex had been overhauled and a new One World Trade Center erected, the state of New York and specifically Governor Andrew Cuomo, forgot. The governor turned One World Trade Center into another symbol, even if only for a night, as the tower was illuminated in the color pink to celebrate the New York State Legislature's passing of "The Reproductive Health Act" which expanded abortion rights throughout the state. The legislation decriminalized abortion and removed most of the restrictions on abortions after 24 weeks (the point where most babies are viable outside of the womb). Furthermore, the bill also granted midwives and nurse practitioners the right to perform abortions.

Gov. Cuomo was quoted in the *Washington Times*:

> *The Reproductive Health Act is a historic victory for New Yorkers and for our progressive values. In the face of a federal government intent on rolling back Roe v. Wade and women's reproductive rights, I promised that we would enact this critical legislation within the first 30 days of the new session – and we got it done. I am directing that New York's landmarks be lit in pink to celebrate this achievement and shine a bright light forward for the rest of the nation to follow.*

A symbol and memorial for those mercilessly killed on 9/11 became a proclamation of more merciless killings under the guise of reproductive health. Something has gone awry in America when we allow not only the execution of babies, but we also begin to celebrate it. Unfortunately, the legislative war on life in 2019, didn't end in New York but spread to Maine, Nevada, Louisiana, Vermont, Virginia, the Supreme Court and the U.S. Senate.

Democratic State Delegate Kathy Tran brought Virginia's proposed legislation to the floor which would allow abortion up to the moment of birth. Testifying before the Virginia floor, she was asked incredulously, multiple times by Republican Majority Leader Todd Gilbert, what the limit was to her proposed legislation.

He asked specifically, "Where it's obvious that a woman is about to give birth, she has physical signs that she's about to give birth, would that still be a point at which she could request an abortion if she was so certified?" In conclusion, Tran answered calmly without flinching, "I don't think we have a limit in the bill. My bill would allow that. Yes."

The prophet Jeremiah answers this testimony in Jeremiah 6:15, *"'Were they ashamed when they committed abomination? No, they were not at all ashamed; they did not know how to blush. Therefore they shall fall among those who fall; at the time that I punish them, they shall be overthrown,' says the Lord."*

These legislative actions are the result of the slippery slope of devaluing life both in and out of the womb. Convenience and choice have replaced the American values of long-suffering and dignity. We have forgotten our Creator and no longer value the *Imago Dei*. Instead, we are fighting to ascend the throne of the One who created us in His image.

With all of the state fights taking place, Nebraska Senator Ben Sasse introduced a procedural motion to the Senate floor for his proposed legislation, "Born-Alive Abortion Survivors Protection Act." On February 25, 2019, the procedural motion was defeated on the Senate floor by failing to get the 60 votes needed to bring it officially to the floor for a vote – the final vote was 53-44. How incredulous to think that 44 American Senators would vote against a bill that would preserve the life of a baby who survives a botched abortion! Essentially, 44 Senators agreed to the legality of partial birth abortion and even worse--infanticide. These senators all failed to see the value of protecting the innocent lives of newborns who survived the abortion procedure. We no longer declare a baby as a human by the low standard of viability outside of the womb, but clearly we have sunk to a new low and only declare a baby a real life if it's "wanted." What an utterly dangerous and treacherous slippery slope!

Sen. Sasse, speaking on the floor on behalf of his bill said,

> I want to ask each and every one of my colleagues whether we're okay with infanticide. This language is blunt. I recognize that and it's too blunt for many people in this body. But frankly, that is what we're talking about here today. Infanticide is what the Born-Alive Abortion Survivors Protection Act is actually about. Are we a country that protects babies that are alive, born outside the womb after having survived a botched abortion? That is what this is about. Are we a country that says it's okay to actively allow that baby to die, which is the current position of federal law? That's the question before us, plain and simple. ... Despite opposition and setbacks, despite some strange rhetoric about this bill over the course of the last week, I am hopeful in the long term. Deep down, each of us knows that every member of our human family ought to be protected, and deserves to be cherished and loved. The love we see every day in the eyes of moms and dads for their newborn babies is an inescapable reminder of that fundamental truth. Love is stronger than power.

After the defeat of the procedural motion, Senator Patty Murray of Washington decried the legislation as "clearly anti-doctor, anti-woman, and anti-family. It has no place becoming law. Its proponents claim it would make something illegal that is already illegal. It would do nothing except help Republicans advance their goal of denying women their constitutionally protected rights."

Leana Wen, then president of Planned Parenthood Federation of America, said, "We must call out today's vote for what it is: a direct attack on women's health and rights. This legislation is based on lies and a misinformation campaign, aimed at shaming women and criminalizing doctors for a practice that doesn't exist in medicine or reality."

Brothers and sisters, we cannot win the fight for life in the courtroom, in the legislatures of our states, or in the halls of the U.S. Congress until we win the battle in the hearts and minds of the people made in the image of God.

We must act through the example of our lives. The truth is we don't just need the U.S. government to defund Planned Parenthood or make new laws against abortion. We need our hearts changed and our deeds altered so that our lives defund Planned Parenthood and make abortion unthinkable. Church, what would happen if we got to know the family next door? What would happen if we stopped running our kids to endless activities and freed our schedules to get involved in the lives of pregnant women, children in foster care and their families, and orphans and their families?

We need to stop wasting our lives on Facebook and social media and instead invest our lives in gospel transformation and discipleship. Are we ready for the Supreme Court of the United States of America to make abortion illegal? Are our churches ready not just to promote birth, but to help women raise their children for life? When a pregnant woman can't parent, are we prepared to counsel her and present the adoption option? Will we be willing and ready to stand in the gap? Will we open our homes to adoption and foster care? Will we use our time to be mentors and disciple makers? Beloved, are we really willing to let the gospel reclaim our families?

May our lives not be wasted but be spent for the gospel! And may the gospel displayed in our lives show the mercy and grace of our Lord Jesus, that while we were still sinners, Christ came and became our sacrifice.

What else must we do? We must pray. The current climate should move us from our seat of judgment onto our knees in prayer for the defense of life and the trajectory of our country and our world.

A dear friend commented on these aforementioned bills shortly after they were introduced. She said, "My soul weeps. ... I cannot even fathom this. As a woman who bore a child from rape and has been unbelievably blessed by him, I cannot conceive of such evil. But having also been in an unplanned pregnancy, I know how crafty the enemy is. ... I know how easy it is to believe his lies. ... only because of the abundant grace of God, my son is here. I was weak even as a believer, so my heart breaks for those who don't yet know Him. I am praying without ceasing!"

And beloved, this is exactly what we need to do – pray without ceasing. Here is a guide that will lead you in prayer for ten days. Be encouraged to use this, add to it as the Lord leads, and put it on repeat until the Lord returns.

Beloved, are you ready to stand in the gap?

Ten Days of Prayer

DAY ONE | Pray for a softening of the hearts of U.S. governors, state lawmakers, and Congress to the gospel. Pray for them to see babies in the womb and their mothers as valuable people made in the image of God.

DAY TWO | Pray for women around the world who feel as if they have no other option than to end the life of their unborn child.

DAY THREE | Pray for the fathers of unborn children. Pray that they will encourage women to choose life for their child and that they would get involved with appropriate support for life.

DAY FOUR | Pray for the Church. Pray that she will be able to show love and compassion to women in unexpected pregnancies. Pray that she will continue this love and compassion after the birth of the child, and even after an abortion decision.

DAY FIVE | Pray for the Christ-exalting pregnancy resource centers throughout the U.S. and the world. Pray for their protection, and pray that women in unexpected pregnancies will be connected with them.

DAY SIX | Pray for the abortion providers in the U.S. and around the world. Pray for their salvation and for their eyes to be opened to the precious lives they are seeking to abort.

DAY SEVEN | Pray for those providing abortion recovery services. Pray that women will connect to them and they will learn about forgiveness and redemption through Christ.

DAY EIGHT | Pray for OBGYNs. Pray that the pro-life OBGYNs will flourish and women will be led divinely to these practices.

DAY NINE | Pray that the Lord will use whatever means necessary to give women truthful information about the adoption option.

DAY TEN | Pray that, in God's miraculous way, women will connect with Lifeline Children's Services and other Christ exalting adoption pregnancy counseling ministries so that we will have an opportunity to share the gospel with them.

Life is Not a Choice

We must recognize, life is not a choice. *For by Him all things were created, in heaven and on earth, visible and invisible, whether thrones or dominions or rulers or authorities — all things were created through Him and for Him. And He is before all things, and in Him all things hold together* (Colossians 1:16-17). Every life is a masterpiece, and as believers, we are losing the abortion battle because our battlefield has become limited to the courtroom and the halls of government instead of extending to the hearts and souls of men. Our messaging is stale and lacking passion for the Creator. We have made women in crisis the villains instead of seeing them as the mission field. Our rhetoric marks pro-choice advocates as evil, instead of dropping to our knees in prayer for their souls, hearts, and minds to be turned to our great God.

Our failure to honor God through valuing the *Imago Dei* has ramifications far beyond the shores of the U.S. According to the Guttmacher Institute, an average of 56 million children are lost to abortion each year worldwide. In fact, one in four of all pregnancies across the world end in abortion. The vast nature of this global genocide is staggering. Though abortion rates have dropped incrementally in recent years, we are far from winning the fight for life.

We are losing the battle for life in the hearts and minds of people not just because our messaging is poor. We are losing because we have lost the zest that the Lord intended for us to have. It is uber exciting to be a part of the pro-life movement, and we don't need large marketing firms to define slogans and talking points; we simply need to turn to the Bible with fervor. God's Word is full of adventure, full of life, and full of an exhilarating pursuit. Our Savior gives us the only talking points we need when He tells us in John 10:10-11, *"The thief comes only to steal and kill and destroy. I came that they may have life and have it abundantly. I am the good shepherd. The good shepherd lays down His life for the sheep."*

Jesus didn't lay down His life in order for us to live boring, stuffy lives with dull messages but to live a full life, faithfully defending His image bearers while preaching the good news of the Kingdom. Each life that the Lord fashions in the womb bears His image and has a distinct purpose.

Beloved, abortion is scary. Abortion is evil because it eliminates a life that is rich, meaningful, and purposeful in Christ. When we push back evil with the light of the gospel, we can expect that the darkness will strike back and attack. However, our response to these attacks on the Kingdom of Light must be to respond with the love of Christ.

The Apostle Paul gives a beautiful exposition of the love that abhors evil in his epistle to the Church at Rome.

Let love be genuine. Abhor what is evil; hold fast to what is good. Love one another with brotherly affection. Outdo one another in showing honor. Do not be slothful in zeal, be fervent in spirit, serve the Lord. Rejoice in hope, be patient in tribulation, be constant in prayer. Contribute to the needs of the saints and seek to show hospitality. Bless those who persecute you; bless and do not curse them. Rejoice with those who rejoice, weep with those who weep. Live in harmony with one another. Do not be haughty, but associate with the lowly. Never be wise in your own sight. Repay no one evil for evil, but give thought to do what is honorable in the sight of all. If possible, so far as it depends on you, live peaceably with all. Beloved, never avenge yourselves, but leave it to the wrath of God, for it is written, "Vengeance is mine, I will repay, says the Lord." To the contrary, "If your enemy is hungry, feed him; if he is thirsty, give him something to drink; for by so doing you will heap burning coals on his head." Do not be overcome by evil, but overcome evil with good. —**Romans 12:9-21**

Today, unfortunately, I believe we spend less time fighting abortion on our knees in prayer and with our lives through discipleship and more time in the public square of social media including Twitter, Facebook, Instagram, (and all of those I don't know about yet). While these outlets can be fantastic tools, they also can drive our pride, remove our filter, and urge a hateful rhetoric. We say things on social media we would never say to someone when face-to-face, and honestly, it can make things more about us than about the message and mission. Rarely, do I see anyone post anything on social media that would make him look weak, foolish, or self-deprecating. Even on those occasions when we show our frailty, we tend to craft our posts in such a way as to make us look humble or pitied. What would happen if we dropped our social media crusades and redirected our time and energy into real engagement with real people about the sanctity of lives?

Practical Steps

We cannot miss that the fight is not a fight merely of words and legal actions, but it is from the sweat of our brow by supporting our rhetoric with the way that we love the orphan, the single mom, the woman who made an adoption plan, the family who has lost their children to the foster care system, and those image bearers who are plagued with a special need or disability. We must expand our focus on issues of life to have a whole-life message and show the world that we love pregnant women as much as we love their children and trust that little by little the Spirit will draw more people in to listen to our full message of life. When we are waiting on the other end of the maternity ward to embrace a single mom and her child, that is the moment we begin to show with our lives and actions how much we truly value life.

Please do not miss it: all of these actions are not merely occasions to deal with earthly distress. They all make great opportunities for gospel proclamation because when we love life tangibly, we receive extraordinary opportunities to speak of the greatest pro-life advocate, Jesus, the One who gave His life so that we could truly have life.

The time has come for the army of light that is committed to the gospel of Jesus Christ to push back the oppression, brutality, and homicide of abortion. Every believer, no matter their gifting, can do something. We need believers to be judges, legislators, and government officials to advocate for policies to fund alternatives to abortion and policies that will make abortion illegal. We also need women who are called according to the grace of the Lord Jesus to volunteer and staff crisis pregnancy centers, love women in crisis with the love of Christ, and wrap around them with tangible support.

Likewise, we need creative people who can help rebrand crisis pregnancy centers to compete with the services of Planned Parenthood. Instead of merely fighting for and praying for the defunding of Planned Parenthood, we need to open pregnancy centers that consistently offer comprehensive women's health services including cancer screenings and provide resources for women. When crisis pregnancy centers are robust and can provide a full range of health services for women, then the argument for funding Planned Parenthood diminishes as their lone distinctive as an abortion provider.

Christian moms have a place at the table to end abortion by inviting struggling young moms into their homes and lives to mentor and disciple these young women and to show them a model of a godly mom. Christian men are needed to fill roles vacated by absent fathers and to reclaim responsibility for the strength, leadership, and integrity of the masculine.

Men, we have to step up and realize that abortion is not just a woman's issue. Abortion is equally a man's issue. If Christian men would "man up," lead, love, and nurture our families and women, then we could easily see a reverse in the devastating trend of abortion. Our God has created men and women distinctly unique. He has created us purposefully. Men and women give and receive love in different ways. Men, we need to love these precious helpmates the way they were designed to receive love, not in a way that serves our physical desire.

I love what Dr. David Platt of McLean Bible Church in Washington, D.C., says in his book *Counter Culture: Following Christ in an Anti-Christian Age:*

> *This means, husbands, that you and I don't love our wives based upon what we get from them. That's how the world defines love in marriage. The world says that you love your wife because of all her attractive attributes and compelling characteristics, but this is a dangerously fickle love. For as soon as some attribute or characteristic fades, then love fails. Husbands, love your wives not because of who they are, but because of who Christ is. He loves them deeply, and our responsibility is to reflect His love.*

Dads, let's teach single men that true love is truly a love that waits. And let's pray over young single men and teach them the wisdom from the Proverbs and other parts of the Word of God because the Bible is both true and utterly practical. Let's not only reprove young men with the Word, but let's also take it to heart ourselves and lead by example in the way we love our wives, are faithful to our families, and respect our daughters.

Solomon instructs men,

> *Do not desire her beauty in your heart, and do not let her capture*
> *you with her eyelashes; for the price of a prostitute is only a loaf of*
> *bread, but a married woman hunts down a precious life. Can a man*
> *carry fire next to his chest and his clothes not be burned? Or can one*
> *walk on hot coals and his feet not be scorched? So is he who goes*
> *in to his neighbor's wife; none who touches her will go unpunished.*
> — **Proverbs 6:25-29**

And then in the Song of Solomon we see this sage advice,

> *I adjure you, O daughters of Jerusalem, by the gazelles or the does*
> *of the field, that you not stir up or awaken love until it pleases.*
> — **Song of Solomon 2:7**

If men would love women with a protective love, guard their hearts, and be committed to staying pure and chaste, I believe the abortion debate would grow very small and insignificant. Let us not be fooled; the sexual revolution of today came from a Church that became biblically illiterate. To see the culture change, we need the Word of God to once again be the cornerstone of our homes and our lives because family has always been God's primary setting for discipleship. God directed Israel to keep His Word upon their hearts by consistently teaching their children in the context of daily life.

> *You shall teach them diligently to your children, and shall talk of*
> *them when you sit in your house, and when you walk by the way, and*
> *when you lie down, and when you rise. You shall bind them as a sign*
> *on your hand, and they shall be as frontlets between your eyes. You*
> *shall write them on the doorposts of your house and on your gates.*
> — **Deuteronomy 6:7-9**

If we follow suit and diligently teach our children God's Word and embrace covenant faithfulness in marriage, we are pushing back against the tide of abortion.

Finally, we need Christians to help fund the movement and be committed to extending support to what is sure to be a long, arduous battle. Until our Lord comes back, we will have some form of abortion, brokenness, disease, famine, sword, and sin. As a result, we will continue to wrestle against a devaluation of life, children in foster care, orphans, widows, and struggling families. If we are going to be there as the Church to fill the gap, we must have resources for the fight including our funds, our time, our comfort, and our voice.

If our churches truly embrace a pro-life ethic and start mentoring broken families, children with special needs, drug addicts, and those with lives marred by sin; then our churches, nurseries, small groups, and children's ministries are going to become very different. If we demonstrate that all people are made in the image of God, our churches are going to become very different. I hope and pray that churches will increasingly look as diverse as Heaven will look one day. As church members, we must give to support work that reflects Kingdom diversity instead of giving to support a Church that looks just like us. We must give and work toward a Church that includes all whom Jesus shed His blood to redeem. Only a Church like that will make a huge dent in eliminating abortion.

Discussion Questions

1. How has "survival of the fittest" thinking influenced our understanding of the *Imago Dei*?

2. Think back to the illustration of a preborn child to a masterpiece. How can this line of thinking change your conversations about abortion?

3. Displaying love for vulnerable people and those with special needs can be a powerful way to affirm the *Imago Dei*. How can these actions be part of our strategy to combat abortion?

4. What are some practical ways you and your church can love vulnerable people in Jesus' name?

5. Can you identify some trustworthy ministries who care for orphans, women in unexpected pregnancies, widows, or struggling families? How can you help with the time, talent and treasure that God has entrusted to you?

Chapter Three
TRULY PRO-LIFE

*...one erects a statue of Stalin because you want to look at Stalin and
think about Stalin. You put up a statue of George Washington to be
reminded of the founding fathers. Images are made to image.
What does this mean for flesh and blood? It means God created little
images of Himself so that they would talk and act
and feel in a way that reveals the way God is.*

— John Piper

This question that confronts us: "Are we willing to be inconvenienced in order to defend life?"

We truly have become a people who want to be entertained, want levels of comfort, and want bite-sized opportunities that will not be a huge inconvenience to our goals and plans.

One of the hardest things about getting our hands dirty in the pro-life movement is that it requires real life engagement not just photo ops or opportunities to make a splash on social media. Being truly pro-life changes the way we look at everyday life and how we invest our time in the lives of the broken and hurting around us.

It is necessary for us to be passionate proponents of life in the womb—we must be a voice for the voiceless. We must counsel women going through unplanned pregnancies to preserve the lives of the unborn. We must lobby and pray for laws and lawmakers who understand the sanctity of life of the unborn; however, our advocacy, our passion, and our ethics must be so much more robust than just being against abortion.

Rightly, we see abortion as murder and an affront against our Creator, but we must also see our apathy against the injustices toward life beyond the womb as the great co-conspirator against our fight for life.

Let me illustrate. In January 2019, I received a call from a friend and ministry partner in Birmingham, Alabama. Eric is an attorney who uses his practice to protect religious organizations and churches as well as to fight for laws that would eliminate abortion and value all life. Eric requested that I personally and Lifeline corporately support a new bill that he was introducing to the Alabama State Congress which would make abortion a felony for those practitioners who perform the procedure.

Instantly, we joined the team by writing testimony which showed that there are families who are willing to adopt an influx of children should the law pass. Also, I was asked to testify in person before both chambers in order to establish that as a State we had the resources and ability to bring services for women and children. This law was written to establish personhood of the unborn baby and was believed on a national level to be a legitimate bill which could sufficiently challenge Roe v. Wade.

By God's grace and mercy, even with lots of national attention and local fights, Alabama's Governor Kay Ivey signed the bill into law on May 15, 2019. The backlash instantly began. Saturday Night Live departed from their normal farce-type humor and brought a five-minute tirade against the bill. Los Angeles banned travel for government officials to Alabama. On opposing sides, U.S. politicians voiced their opinions.

American lawyer, politician and junior U.S. Senator from California, Kamala Harris (who was running for the 2020 Presidential bid), spoke out against the bill:

> Those folks down in Alabama who are doing this, these are the same folks who, by the time that baby is born, they couldn't care less. What are they doing to support that mother and what she needs in terms of prenatal help? They're not doing a thing, but they're trying to tell women what to do with their bodies. We're going to tell them a thing or two.

The sad reality is that while Sen. Harris is misguided on her views from a biblical worldview, she does speak some important truth. As a whole, our churches are not stepping up to support single mothers, drug addicts, and the older teens trapped in foster care. Our churches are homogeneous racial havens that provide a safe retreat from the culture as opposed to aggressive tapestries of grace which give the gospel as the only antidote to society's woes.

If we truly have a pro-life ethic that values the *Imago Dei*, then we will exemplify and follow the model of Christ that Paul laid out to the church at Philippi:

> Do nothing from selfish ambition or conceit, but in humility count others more significant than yourselves. Let each of you look not only to his own interests, but also to the interests of others. Have this mind among ourselves, which is yours in Christ Jesus, who, though He was in the form of God, did not count equality with God a thing to be grasped, but emptied Himself, by taking the form of a servant, being born in the likeness of men. And being found in human form, He humbled Himself by becoming obedient to the point of death, even death on a cross. — **Philippians 2:3-8**

I ask people all the time, what will our talking points be if, by God's grace, abortion is made illegal? What action will we take? The answer to these questions identifies if we are really pro-life or if we are just pro-birth. Will men step up and get off their smartphones and stop amusing themselves to death and join their wives in caring for the single mom in their sphere of influence to show her and her children a positive male role model? Will we be willing to sacrifice our time to mentor a woman or family that is in crisis and has lost children into State custody because of addiction, poverty, or poor decisions?

Are we willing, no matter our stage of life, to use our home to foster children while they are displaced from their homes? Will we adopt children from the foster care system, from American women who need to place their babies instead of parent, or children from other countries? Are we open to adopt these children no matter their past trauma, no matter their special need, and no matter their age?

You see, being pro-life is not just about eliminating abortion. Being pro-life means putting our families into action to live out our passion for guarding the *Imago Dei*.

Here is an example of the kind of thing that I mean. In November 2013, Lifeline's Domestic Education Manager, Traci Newell, bound into my office with her usual energy and pizzazz. She saw a serious need in foster care: to help families seeking to be reunified with their children. She wanted Lifeline to begin offering the state approved parenting class to families who had lost their children to the foster care system. The idea was to train 10 to 15 families a year from the Birmingham Metro area in our office. We would use the state training core but infuse it with the gospel and biblical parenting.

Well, our sweet Jesus took that idea and did infinitely more than we could have ever imagined. Instead of our staff offering the training, the Lord multiplied the program through local churches offering the classes. This program, Families Count, has spread to over seven states in its first four years of existence with more than 30 church partners holding classes. The Lord has used this simple gospel-saturated class in such profound ways that several denominations are trying to offer Families Count through churches in every state.

The program involves parenting classes that are offered one night a week for six weeks, hosted by local churches, and taught by a couple in that church.

The core of the class is comprised of believers from these local churches who provide the participants with weekly meals, transportation, and relationships. Families Count is designed to create long-lasting mentor and discipleship relationships between these broken families and the local church.

Here is the wonderful thing: Families Count is significantly outperforming similar programs, and we are convinced it is because the Church is bringing the gospel to bear. We have seen story after story of life transformation. We have seen moms and dads thriving as they are reunified with their kids. Of utmost importance, these families are being introduced to their Lord and Savior.

I think about one family in particular. We will call them "Cal" and "Trish." I had the opportunity to spend some time with Cal and Trish and hear their story. As a result of an unplanned pregnancy and limited finances, they married just out of high school. As they kept having children, job opportunities to support their growing family became fewer and fewer. Finally, they gave into mounting pressure and succumbed to addiction.

As Cal and Trish's addiction grew, their relationship crumbled, their parenting fell into ruins, and they gave way to neglect. After multiple reports of gross neglect and cruelty, the State of Alabama did what it has been chartered to do and took Cal and Trish's children into State custody. Throughout this downward spiral, only the goal of being reunified with their children captured this couple's attention. Through the court's efforts to help them seek reunification with their children, they first learned about Families Count.

Trish told me that they hatched a plan. Cal was sleeping on the couch, and they really had no intention of becoming a family again. Instead, they thought they would do just enough to be reunited with their kids. Once reunified, they planned to get a divorce because they hated one another.

Time came for them to attend the first class at a local church in their town. The county office for Child Protective Services added an unexpected wrinkle to the plan. Child welfare officials decided that they would combine Cal and

Trish's visitation with their children with their attendance at Families Count. What happened next is simply a move of the Spirit through His people humbly serving Cal and Trish and their family.

The first way that this church served this family was by treating them with dignity and a family meal together by including them in the church's regular Wednesday night meal. A simple act of kindness meant a great deal to this hurting family, and God was using the church in even deeper ways too. As Cal and Trish attended the class, their four kids joined the church's programs for children. After the first night, the oldest child told her parents, "I met Jesus tonight and surrendered my life to Him."

Trish told me that she thought that was sweet, but she just wanted to finish the class; however, as her kids were taken back to their foster parents, their daughter told her mom and dad that they needed Jesus too. Wow!

One of the other ways the church was ministering to them was by providing mentors to meet with them weekly and to pray with them. Trish asked the mentor family assigned to them what all of this meant and what did Jesus have to do with their torn apart family? Trish felt as though all God had ever done for her was to disappoint her and let her down. The mentor couple felt led by the Holy Spirit to challenge Cal and Trish to go home and read the Book of James. Through His sovereignty, God spoke to this broken couple through the words that James wrote under the Holy Spirit's inspiration millennia ago.

After class on week two of Families Count, Cal and Trish surrendered their lives to Christ with their mentor couple. Fast forward three years, Cal and Trish are reunified with their kids, are members of this church and in a small group, and are helping with the leadership team with Families Count. Also, through the bold witness of Cal and Trish, more than ten members of their extended family have come to saving faith in Christ. Members of their church even helped Cal and Trish secure jobs to provide for their family.

Brothers and sisters, this is an example of being truly, holistically pro-life.

A Generational Shift

I believe the Millennial generation gets a pretty bad rap at times, and I want to commend them for two significant positive trends. First, they are the most pro-life generation alive today. I believe this is because science has finally caught up with God, and the images now seen through ultrasounds have the power to show that a life within a mother's womb begins to live at conception. Second, Millennials are willing to adopt, foster, and advocate for orphaned and vulnerable children en masse. I love how many married Millennial couples are looking toward adoption and foster care before even thinking about pregnancy. They are getting engaged with adoption and foster care because of a passionate calling, not just because of infertility.

The call to value orphaned and vulnerable children as created in the image of God is not merely a call to Millennials. We need to get all living generations involved in a truly pro-life movement because they each have unique things to offer. To involve all generations in the movement, we must first learn how to deliver information to engage each one in ways that make the movement accessible and tangible.

Younger generations may prefer Instagram or other forms of social media. Older generations may be more likely to read a newsletter or something they receive in their mailbox. My Baby Boomer mother-in-law consistently brings newsletters and articles highlighted with impactful things she wants to bring to our attention. My Gen-X peers text me links to articles. The Millennials on my team find a picture speaks a thousand words.

No matter the communication style, we must have entry ramps for all people to get engaged and involved, and with our messaging we have to give a full, honest picture by showing success while giving a true expectation of the struggles. We must celebrate the adoption of a child with Down syndrome or a teenager from the foster system; however, we must also make it known that raising these children is challenging and exhausting.

While Millennials are the generation most engaged in caring for children through adoption and foster care, older generations can support them financially, prayerfully, and with wisdom. Older generations usually have the gift of more flexible schedules that allow them to come alongside the families of children from hard places to mentor, volunteer, and serve. Younger generations have reckless abandon mixed with idealism, while older generations have the sage wisdom to help shape the calling into a bold mission.

I urge you to leverage all that God has blessed you with—time, talent, and treasure—to stand in the gap for all lives. We have yet to see what the Lord can do through His whole Church being totally yielded to a holistic pro-life lifestyle.

Life Counts Amid Tragedy

On Sunday, November 5, 2017, Devin Kelley entered into the First Baptist Church of Sutherland, Texas, and began an assault upon the congregation. Depending on which news report you were following or in which state you live, you may have heard a different number for the death toll of this tragic event, and the reason for the difference cuts right to the heart of the struggle to value life.

By Texas law and thus by that state's official count, 27 lives were mercilessly taken on that November Sunday. However, many news sources and states, including California, are only allowing their reporters to promote that 26 lives were lost.

Why the discrepancy? Who represents the single life counted by some and ignored by others? The one counted by the State of Texas as a person was a baby nestled tightly within his mother's womb who lost his life at the same time as his mother.

How can one nation, under God, indivisible, count so differently? The truth is the U.S. has not lost the capacity for basic math, but instead lost its moral fabric. In many states outside of Texas, a life that has not yet thrived outside of the womb is not worthy of being counted. Even worse, in some states the life only counts if the mother "wants" the baby.

Beloved Christ-follower, this stands in direct opposition to the precious Word of God when Isaiah says in Isaiah 44:24, *"Thus says the Lord, your Redeemer, who formed you from the womb: 'I am the Lord, who made all things, who alone stretched out the heavens, who spread out the earth by Myself.'"*

Isaiah also says later in Isaiah 64:8, *"But now, O Lord, you are our Father; we are the clay, and You are our potter; we are all the work of Your hand."*

We are the clay and God is the potter. He does not make pots or instruments that need to be thrown away. He is the author of life, and He is the only one who can determine the beginning and the end of life. This is not a gray matter that we can take into our hands just because we possess the medical technology to do so.

Life is not a choice. Life is precious and a responsibility given by God. We are formed in the image of God; and thus, we are the *Imago Dei*! We bear the mark of God's image in our lives and nothing could be more precious. Why should we advocate for the sanctity of life? Because, like in Texas, all lives count to our God.

Let us be people who heed the call of Proverbs 31:8-9, *"Open your mouth for the mute, for the rights of all who are destitute. Open your mouth, judge righteously, defend the rights of the poor and needy."*

Not to stand up and not to speak up at best means that we are ashamed of the gospel. At worst, it means we do not know the gospel. We must speak for those who cannot speak for themselves. We must value all life, because ultimately, we are a life that Christ valued all the way to the Cross.

Standing for Life is a Call to Justice

You shall appoint judges and officers in all your towns that the LORD your God is giving you, according to your tribes, and they shall judge the people with righteous judgment. You shall not pervert justice. You shall not show partiality, and you shall not accept a bribe, for a bribe blinds the eyes of the wise and subverts the cause of the righteous. Justice, and only justice, you shall follow, that you may live and inherit the land that the LORD your God is giving you.
—**Deuteronomy 16:18-20**

In the Bible, justice is meant to be the process of making things right or as it should be. Before the fall, there was no need for justice, nor will there be a need for justice when the Lord comes to redeem His Creation. However, because sin has marred our world completely, we desperately need justice – this is one of God's attributes and flows out of His holiness. After the fall, the perfect created order became undone, but God in His holiness has invited us to partner with Him in restoring justice. Being pro-life is about being pro-justice because the major affronts of the fallen world are directly against God and those created in His image.

Justice, righteousness, and reconciliation are often used synonymously in the Bible. The world has come undone, and the world is in need to be redeemed by her creator. This is why Paul calls us to be ministers of reconciliation in 2 Corinthians 5:18-21. We are to participate with God in pushing back against the darkness of this fallen world. Paul Lewis Metzger, professor of Christian theology at Multnomah Christian Seminary says,

Biblical justice involves making individuals, communities, and the cosmos whole, by upholding both goodness and impartiality. It stands at the center of true religion, according to James, who says that the kind of "religion that God our Father accepts as pure and faultless is this: to look after orphans and widows in their distress and to keep oneself from being polluted by the world" (James 1:27). Earlier

Scripture says, "The righteous care about justice for the poor, but the wicked have no such concern" (Prov. 29:7).

Because we are ambassadors of reconciliation, instruments of God's justice, and those who crave the righteousness of God, we must understand that the call to defend life, is a call to justice in the world.

Discussion Questions

1. Recognizing that being "pro-life" is more than just desiring to eliminate abortion, how has that changed your understanding of the term?

2. How does Philippians 2:3-8 speak into our call as Christ-followers to guard the *Imago Dei*? What are some ways you can abide in this passage as someone who is "pro-life"?

3. Considering the ways different generations can holistically care for life, how do you see opportunities for your small group, your kids, or your parents to work together to minister to others?

4. How does knowing you're representing and partnering with a holy God in this pro-justice movement change the rhetoric you use when speaking or posting about being "pro-life"?

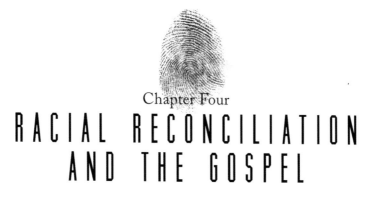

Chapter Four

RACIAL RECONCILIATION
AND THE GOSPEL

But you are a chosen race, a royal priesthood, a holy nation, a people
for His own possession, that you may proclaim the excellencies of
Him who called you out of darkness into His marvelous light.
Once you were not a people, but now you are God's people;
once you had not received mercy, but now you have received mercy.

— 1 Peter 2:9-10

Many years before Trayvon Martin, Michael Brown, Alton Sterling, Philando Castile, and countless others were slain, there was One who willingly laid down His life. The Lamb of God was slain so that by His blood we would be healed and made a people—a holy race. This race is one made of all skin tones, languages, nations, and tribes.

Jesus the Christ died to reconcile every people group from our nasty, filthy sin into His holy and perfect life. It's by His wounds that we find true healing. *So God created man in His own image, in the image of God He created him; male and female He created them.* (Genesis 1:27)

The U.S. needs healing, and we need a recalibration of our moral compass. America has forsaken her true love. Battles are being lost in the courtroom. Elections have become contests between candidates who have forgotten how to blush (Jeremiah 6:15). Americans worry more about the economy than ethics and honesty. Ultimately, we are battling each other in the streets because we have lost the truth of *Imago Dei*—that we are all made in the image of God (Genesis 1:26-27).

Bombs explode in Turkey and Iraq, and the stories barely make our news feed. Radicals gun down the image bearers of God in Orlando and Southern California, and we pause only long enough to condemn the other image bearers responsible for these heinous atrocities. Dear Christ-follower, our nation and our world need the restorative hope that comes only in the victorious and death-defying power of Jesus.

And, beloved brother and sister in Christ, we have viewed racial reconciliation as a social issue and not a gospel issue. The truth is our bloodlines are not skin deep but run down deep into our souls. Our brothers and sisters are dark chocolate, pearly white, and all shades in between. We are a kaleidoscope of the creativity of our Father. We are image bearers of our Daddy! Christ died to redeem us as one united race under the banner of Jesus the Christ of Nazareth! Our responsibility as image bearers requires us to seek gospel driven justice through wholeness, fairness, and racial equality.

The gospel is so beautiful as it weaves a tapestry of grace throughout all people groups, all ethoses, and all shades of skin as we are reminded that we are no longer slaves to sin but sons and daughters of Almighty God. As sons, yes even as heirs of the Almighty, our mission is to go into all cultures, nations, races, neighborhoods, regions, and religions to proclaim the excellencies of the gospel of the Kingdom of our Daddy. *Rejoice with those who rejoice, weep with those who weep. (Romans 12:15)*

So believer, there is no excuse not to weep with those who weep and to mourn with those who mourn in Baton Rouge, Louisiana; Falcon Heights, Minnesota; Dallas, Texas; and every corner of this country and this world where the lives of image bearers of our Father are lost. The gospel shows us the depth, height, and breadth of God's love, which reaches into the inner city ghettos, through the gated communities of prestige, through the heart of the Middle East, and ultimately throughout all nations.

We need to show compassion before judgment and empathy before blame as we engage in racial reconciliation. We need to slay our self-righteous pride, which places our safety, our personal security, and ourselves at the center of the world. Paul David Tripp, in his daily devotional, *New Morning Mercies*, says, "God is at the center of His universe, and when you put yourself there, it only ends in relational brokenness and personal disappointment."

Beloved Christ-follower, especially my caucasian brothers and sisters in the U.S., when it comes to the issue of racial reconciliation, we have put ourselves squarely at the center of the universe and refused to move. We are guilty of what Jesus accuses the Pharisees in Luke.

> But woe to you Pharisees! For you tithe mint and rue and every herb, and neglect justice and the love of God. These you ought to have done, without neglecting the others. Woe to you Pharisees! For you love the best seat in the synagogues and greetings in the marketplaces.
> —Luke 11:42-32

We want to believe that racism, ethnocentrism, and superiority/privilege are a thing of the past. We neglect the feelings, hurts, and realities of our brothers and sisters who are blessed to have more pigment in their epidermis. However, the truth is we are blind to the sin in our hearts and deaf to the hurts and pains of those around us.

My good friend and brother, James Sutton, hit me one day with a truth that was harder than a two-by-four straight between by eyes, but it was the wound of a brother and a rebuke I desperately needed. I had been discussing recent police shootings of African Americans throughout the U.S. I remember making the comment that would break his heart and bring forth my rebuke.

"But James, we have to trust the police and know that they are here to protect us. They won't be able to do their job and could even bring upon greater harm if they have to hesitate and consider if they are racially profiling," I commented.

With articulation which I could never match, James reminded me that it was the police who had enforced Jim Crowe laws and had sprayed African Americans with fire hydrants in my hometown of Birmingham. He explained how my white son could carry a toy gun in the front yard of my house and never once have the police called upon him, when just a few miles away his black son would rouse immediate suspicion at an innocent game of cops and robbers in the front yard. "Herbie, you are completely blind to your own privilege. Just yesterday I entered into an elevator, smiled at a white woman only to see her clutch her purse and look away," James remarked.

This interaction scared me in a good way. I remember that night laying in bed and weeping to the point that I left the bed so that I wouldn't awaken my wife. I prayed that God would break my heart for racial reconciliation and to forgive me of my blatant satisfaction in the status quo.

Stepping Into a Multicultural World

For You formed my inward parts; You knitted me together in my mother's womb. I praise You, for I am fearfully and wonderfully made. Wonderful are Your works; my soul knows it very well.
—Psalm 139:13-14

One of many gospel-driven steps toward engagement in racial reconciliation involves orphan care, foster care, and adoption. Our families, our lives, and our perspectives change when we step into these multi-cultural worlds. We no longer see people as projects, but we see them as image bearers of Christ who eagerly desire and need authentic relationships.

When we begin the journey to care for the fatherless, the vulnerable, and the widow, we enter a journey into the heart of God for a kingdom and a people of all socio-economic levels, all races, all cultures, all nations, and all languages. Cross-cultural adoptive and foster families soon learn the complexities and realities of the sins of racism, bigotry, resentment, and prejudice. These families quickly begin to understand that the Kingdom of God is more precious because it is only in our Father's family that the differences in our epidermis are truly celebrated.

My friend Jeremy Haskins, a pastor at Ashland Avenue Baptist Church in Lexington, Kentucky, recently wrote a blog post about processing racially charged events with his black and white sons. He writes, "Because they are brothers, racism isn't a social issue. It's a family issue. May it be the same for the family of God. Local churches ought to be the go to place for the world to see what racial reconciliation and familial love that transcends skin color looks like."

Within God's great economy Black Lives Matter, Babies Lives in the Womb Matter, People with Down Syndrome Matter, Babies Born-With-Only-A-Brain-Stem Lives Matter, Elderly Lives Matter, Prostitutes Lives Matter, and All Lives Matter because we are created in the *Imago Dei* — the very image of God. I am truly afraid that the church of Christ has conveniently elevated all other lives above the lives of our black brothers and sisters. While we may see progress because schools and public places are desegregated; if we are honest, our hearts, minds, and spirits are still very much segregated.

> *Within God's great economy Black Lives Matter, Babies Lives in the Womb Matter, People with Down Syndrome Matter, Babies Born-With-Only-A-Brain-Stem Lives Matter, Elderly Lives Matter, Prostitutes Lives Matter, and All Lives Matter because we are created in the Imago Dei — the very image of God.*

Beloved, let's make sure that we read Psalm 139 completely and in context. Psalm 139 is not just a pro-birth passage reminding us that the Lord fashioned us and knew us in our mother's womb. Psalm 139 is about a God from whom we cannot ever hide and who values life as precious both inside the womb and beyond.

Brother and sister in Christ, I beg and plead with you, let's care as much about life that has been born as we do about life in the womb. Love, minister, and speak truth in love to the woman contemplating abortion. Reach out a hand to the 14-year-old who has been displaced from his mom for years, is rebelling against his foster family, and who could wreak havoc to your world. Embrace the uniqueness of a child with cerebral palsy from Asia who may never be able to speak the words "thank you" or "I love you." Adopt a child from a different ethnicity as the Lord leads and show that all life matters because it reflects the glory and image of our Great God.

We are promised that one day our Savior will return, and it is imminent. He will come in all regalia and glory and usher in healing for our world that is broken and torn apart by the curse of sin. Jesus Himself reminds us before His departure, *"I will not leave you as orphans; I will come to you."* What a glorious day that will be. As the old hymn reminds us, "One day the trumpet will sound for His coming, One day the skies with His glories will shine, wonderful day, my Beloved One bringing, My Savior, Jesus ... Oh glorious day, oh glorious day."

Do we yearn for the coming of Jesus or are we more in love with this fallen, sinful world and our ambitions and agendas? Come, Lord Jesus! Come invade us with Your grace, Your gospel, and Your glory. May we spread the seeds of Your Kingdom to reconcile races to You!

It is the responsibility of the Lord's children to show racial reconciliation and the gospel in the distinctive ways that we live our lives. Our lives should reflect our love for the coming Kingdom and in the coming day when as Dr. Martin Luther King, Jr. said "all of God's children, black men and white men, Jews and Gentiles, Protestants and Catholics, will be able to join hands and sing in the words of the old Negro spiritual: 'Free at last. Free at last. Thank God Almighty, we are free at last.'"

*And they sang a new song, saying, "Worthy are You to take the scroll and to open its seals, for You were slain, and by Your blood You ransomed people for God from every tribe and language and people and nation, and You have made them a kingdom and priests to our God, and they shall reign on the earth." —***Revelation 5:9-10**

Beloved, will we allow God to use the gospel through us to impact every shade of image bearer that the Lord has fashioned?

Hate and White Supremacy

Over the weekend of August 16, 2017, in Charlottesville, Virginia, several hate groups touting white supremacy, marched to boycott the city's removal of a statute of Robert E. Lee. This march included a resurgence of the KKK, Neo-Nazis and many other white supremacy groups. As a follower of Christ, we must feel despair that there are still groups that would pit people against each other through racism and ethnocentrism. While this debacle in Charlottesville was certainly not an isolated event of hatred, venom, and racism, we have seen in the U.S., I'm afraid this hate will not be completely eradicated until King Jesus comes to take His rightful reign.

Brothers and sisters, I want us to realize that from cover to cover of God's Word, the Lord repudiates and denounces all forms of racism and ethnocentrism. It is our adversary, the Devil, who brings hatred and animosity between the people created in God's image. Our *"adversary the devil prowls around like a roaring lion, seeking someone to devour"* (1 Peter 5:8) and wants to separate and destroy the image bearers of God.

Beloved white Christian brother or sister, are we guilty in our hearts of racist thoughts and tendencies? Do we dismiss the foster care crisis in our country because its not as prevalent in our zip codes or say that the guilt as a whole for creating children in foster care rests upon a certain race or class of people? Are we guilty of believing that because of the ethnicity of a country or because of their race and culture, they are just prone to having vulnerable children?

We must renounce racism in our own hearts and lay it at the altar of Christ Jesus. I pray that through God's grace we can also erase it from our vernacular and in our churches. Our churches cannot be a refuge of racism, we must preach biblically against it and also make steps to approach humbly our brothers and sisters who have been the victims of our racist pride and superiority.

If racism is in our hearts then we have hatred and vitriol against an image bearer of God. If we don't like diversity, don't appreciate the different skin tones and skin shades that God has created, and don't love the ethnic diversity of our world then we will hate Heaven. Revelation 7:9-10 talks about how God created people groups in order to form His Kingdom—a multiethnic cacophony of praise:

> After this I looked, and behold, a great multitude that no one could number, from every nation, from all tribes and peoples and languages, standing before the throne and before the Lamb, clothed in white robes, with palm branches in their hands, and crying out with a loud voice, "Salvation belongs to our God who sits on the throne, and to the Lamb!"

We are called as God's chosen and holy people to speak up and speak out for the poor, the stranger, the marginalized, and the disenfranchised. Our churches should be a hospice for sinners, allowing them to die to their sin. But our churches should also be an aggressive operating room, looking to confront our deadly sin through the lens of the gospel of the Lord Jesus Christ. May we clearly proclaim and preach that racism is hatred and utterly sinful. May our vernacular begin to inform our actions.

> And He made from one man every nation of mankind to live on all the face of the earth, having determined allotted periods and the boundaries of their dwelling place, that they should seek God, and perhaps feel their way toward Him and find Him. Yet He is actually not far from each one of us, for "In Him we live and move and have our

being;" as even some of your own poets have said, "For we are indeed
His offspring." Being then God's offspring, we ought not to think that
the divine being is like gold or silver or stone, an image formed by
the art and imagination of man. The times of ignorance God over-
looked, but now He commands all people everywhere to repent.
—Acts 17:26-30

Consequently, the first action that we must take in racial reconciliation is
to repent of our sin. We must repent of our racism. We must repent of the
hatred and prejudice that we have in our hearts because it is sin. Then we must
begin to speak out. We must speak out for other people, other tribes, other
languages with different skin tones and skin shades.

Open your mouth for the mute, for the rights of all who are destitute.
Open your mouth, judge righteously, defend the rights of the poor and
needy. —Proverbs 31:8-9

Give justice to the weak and the fatherless; maintain the right of the
afflicted and the destitute. Rescue the weak and the needy; deliver
them from the hand of the wicked. —Psalm 82:3-4

Brothers and sisters, are we appreciating the men and women that are
created in the image of God? As we see other human beings all made uniquely
in God's design, do we realize we are viewing the crown of creation, whom
has been created in the image of God? We must protect the rights and dignity
of all image bearers.

Racism, prejudice, genocide, ethnocentrism, racial superiority and the other
atrocities against the citizens of the world because of their heritage is a full
out assault on the sanctity of human life. We must despise and be as grieved
about racism as we are about abortion, because the issues are the exact
same. Both devalue a person made in God's image.

The spirit of racial superiority which controlled the actions of Adolph Hitler in
Nazi Germany is many times easier for us to see than the same spirit alive in

the hearts and minds of men today. What Hitler did on a broad scale, we are guilty of doing on a small scale each and every day. When Hitler exterminated Jewish people and their sympathizers, the Church stood silent both in America and abroad. And while Hitler has been labeled primarily as a persecutor of the nation of Israel, let it not escape us that Hitler's main objective was a pure Arian race. Hitler locked up the handicapped, he tortured Africans, and he silenced all objectors.

I had the opportunity to go to the Holocaust museum with my sweet wife Ashley in January 2019, while we were in Washington D.C. for a speaking engagement at the Evangelicals for Life conference. We were both silent as we saw references to the genocide and coercion by such an evil dictator. While the pain gripped me, it didn't really become personal until we approached a particular part of the exhibit showing the brutal torture and extermination of those deemed handicapped by the Third Reich. While I was reading and surveying this section, I had the feeling that I was being surrounded by other patrons. I stepped aside to give them a better view when I realized I was surrounded by men, women, boys and girls in wheelchairs, on walkers, and a beautiful young man with Down syndrome. I watched as these precious image bearers wept at the atrocities, and then I stepped into their pain. I was no longer simply angered at the acts of Nazi Germany; I was broken, and it was now personal. In that moment, I was ashamed and grieved that a nation who promoted the superiority of my race had attacked God's image bearers in such a cruel and inhuman way.

Beloved white brother and sister, we must also be grieved with the genocide of racism in our own country. We cannot dismiss the acts of slavery, segregation, and ethnocentrism as bygone days, but we must step into the pain of our brown, tan, and black brothers and sisters. God created all men and women in His image and we should realize that racism is most definitely a sanctity of life issue. Racism, in fact, even fueled the modern day abortion industry in the U.S.

Planned Parenthood and Racism

On April 23, 2017, a column printed by the *Washington Times*, "Planned Parenthood founded on racism, belief in protecting society against 'the unfit,'" quotes many beliefs of the Planned Parenthood celebrated founder, Margaret Sanger. While conservatives today seek to defund Planned Parenthood and make abortion illegal, they fail to be grieved by the racial genocide of this organization.

Research by the U.S. Centers for Disease Control and Prevention (CDC) shows that abortion is the No. 1 cause of death to African Americans in the U.S. today. Around 900 African American babies are aborted every day in the U.S. The Radiance Foundation, created by the National Black Pro-Life Coalition, compiled this data from the CDC from 2008 (the latest aggregated data available). In 2008, there were 286,797 deaths of African Americans broken down by the following causes:

- HIV related deaths — 4,138
- Firearm related deaths — 6,100
- Diabetes related deaths — 12,771
- Accidental deaths — 12,299
- Cancer related deaths — 66,158
- Heart related deaths — 90,888
- Death related to other causes — 94,443

However, in the same year, 317,547 African American babies were aborted in the womb. According to the Guttmacher Institute, known to support abortion, 30% of the total abortions performed in the U.S. in 2011 (1,058,490) were African American babies. However, in the same year the total U.S. population comprised of only 12.1% non-Hispanic blacks. The data shows that African American babies are aborted three times more often than Caucasian babies, and that Hispanic babies are aborted 1.5 times more frequently than Caucasians.

According to the *Washington Times* column, Margaret Sanger founded Planned Parenthood with this mantra:

> *Minorities crammed into impoverished areas in inner cities should not be having so many babies. And, of course, these minorities are inferior in the human race, as are the physically and mentally handicapped. We should require mandatory sterilizations of those less desirable and promote easy access to abortion. And since sex should be a free-for-all, we must provide birth control and abortions to teenagers too. It's all for the greater good and for a more intelligent, liberated, healthier population.*

Furthermore, in her article "A Plan for Peace," Sanger wrote that Planned Parenthood needed, "a stern and rigid policy of sterilization and segregation to that grade of population whose progeny is already tainted, or whose inheritance is such that objectionable traits may be transmitted to offspring."

And then fearing that her racist views would be exposed and could taint the growth of Planned Parenthood, Sanger said in a letter to a partner in 1939, "We do not want a word to go out that we want to exterminate the Negro population."

Beloved, don't miss it. At the heart of the U.S. abortion industry is an outright assault on the sanctity of life outside of the womb, before the agenda ever threatened life inside the womb. The fight for the sanctity of life is not just a concern for the life in the womb. We are concerned for the sanctity of that life once he or she is breathing air no matter their skin color, ethnicity, or disability. We must defend the sanctity of all life, which means the sanctity of life of our Asian brothers and sisters, of our African brothers and sisters, of our Latin American brothers and sisters, and of men and women, red, yellow, black, brown, white and every shade in between. When we speak out against racism, we are defending the sanctity of human life.

We cannot miss another important statistic about black women and childbirth. According to the U.S. Center for Disease Control, black women are three times more likely to die during childbirth. Are we as grieved over this loss of life outside of the womb as we are the loss of life inside the womb? And what if all of those aborted black babies had been born? Would the church have truly shown justice, love, and respect to these children and their mothers?

There are ten ways I believe we are all called to defend the weak, the poor, the widow, the vulnerable, and especially those who are ethnically different from us. I believe we need to start immediately with these ten as we are under attack by an enemy who seeks to infect our hearts with hatred against the *Imago Dei*.

1. We must condemn all forms of racism, genocide, and ethnocentrism and call them sin. It is easier to speak out against groups like ISIS as they are beheading Christians and spewing hate and venom throughout the Middle East. But it is much more difficult to look at ourselves and admit to the racism in our own hearts. It is evil and we must condemn it.

2. We must teach what the Bible says about racism to ourselves, to our children, to our churches, to our neighbors, and to the world. We must be biblically accurate and clear that all men are created in the image of God, and that all men and ethnicities come from one man, Jesus Christ. We must preach that God detests racism.

3. We must repent of the sin of racism and favoritism, whether big or small in our own life. The truth of the matter is, we can't point the finger at others until we point the finger at ourselves. We need to examine our own hearts and address the hatred we find there. Let's repent of the sin of racism and favoritism and remove the log out of our own eye before removing the speck from our brother's.

4. We must drop to our knees and pray. We need to pray for ourselves that we would love one another as image bearers of Christ. We need to pray for our nation that we would repent and turn from the hatred on our streets. We need to pray for our world and for the brutal genocides taking place on every continent. Let us pray toward the day when King Jesus will unite us. Come, Lord Jesus.

5. We must preach the gospel to ourselves and to our neighbors. We desperately need the gospel each and every day. It reminds us who we really are — messy sinners in need of a perfect Savior. Let us preach the gospel to ourselves and then let us preach the gospel to our neighbors. This is the only hope of reconciliation.

6. We must continue speaking against racism, ethnocentrism, genocide, and hatred through the lens of the gospel. It is so easy today to go to social media and give immediate reaction to current events. This medium allows us to tell others what "we think." May we instead use these mediums to speak humbly about racism through the lens of the gospel.

7. We must be passionate and speak out against racism and other sins that creates superiority of one over another in the same way that we speak up for the unborn. These are all equal issues concerning the sanctity of human life.

8. Specifically for my white brothers and sisters or those of use who are in the place of privilege, we must ask our African American brothers and sisters how they are processing the events of racism that we see daily. Let's humbly ask those without privilege how they process the ethnocentrism in our society. Then, with sincerity, let us apologize for what is happening to them and to our world.

9. We must fight the urge to make the sanctity of life a political issue. Let us not become secular in our thinking, caustic with our rhetoric, or identified on all issues by a political party. It is okay to align more from a policy perspective with a political party and to disagree on those alignments with our brothers and sisters. It is never okay to call good evil and evil good all for the sake of our politics. Jesus is our ultimate King and His Kingdom is our real home.

10. We must continue to speak out for the 153 million orphans. Let us continue to speak up for vulnerable children while not belittling their biological families who may have lost their child to foster care because of their poor choices or who may have passed away because of a rough life. Let's never speak down about a child's country of origin or their culture, but instead let's speak with grace about the orphan, their families, their cultures, and their heritage. As God's chosen people, His royal priesthood, and His chosen ones, let us speak up for the rights of others and speak out against injustice. We must embrace diversity because it is the song of Heaven as every tribe, from every people, in every language will stand before the throne of God praising our Savior.

The Lord Will Reunite His People for His Praise

At the Tower of Babel in Genesis Chapter 11, the Lord confuses the language of all people because they were trying to band together to exalt themselves and prove they were higher than the Lord Almighty. God comes onto the scene and creates chaos by confusing their language and thus creating an ethnically diverse people.

I love how Sally Lloyd Jones describes this in her children's Bible, *The Jesus Storybook Bible*. It says,

> One morning, they went to work as usual but everything was different — their words were all new and funny. You see, God had given each person a completely different language! Suddenly, no one understood what anyone else was saying. Someone would say, "How do you do?" and the other person thought they said, "How ugly are you!" It wasn't funny. You could be saying something nice like, "Such a lovely morning!" and get a punch in the nose because they thought you said, "Hush up, you're boring!" (You couldn't even say, "Pardon?" to check if you'd heard right because no one understood that word either.) It wasn't easy to work together after that.

Our adversary was at war with the Creator, and one of His greatest ammunitions was the belief that we could be greater than God — that we could be God. This self reliant pride created the chaos of Babel and then carried on throughout the ages in the form of racial superiority. But our great God has not left us without hope.

> *For at that time I will change the speech of the peoples to a pure speech, that all of them may call upon the name of the Lord and serve Him with one accord. From beyond the rivers of Cush, My worshippers, the daughter of My dispersed ones, shall bring My offering. On that day you shall not be put to shame because of the deeds by which you have rebelled against Me; for then I will remove from your midst your proudly exultant ones, and you shall no longer be haughty in My holy mountain. But I will leave in your midst a people humbleand lowly. They shall seek refuge in the name of the Lord, those who are left in Israel; they shall do no injustice and speak no lies, nor shall there be found in their mouth a deceitful tongue. For they shall graze and lie down, and none shall make them afraid.*
> — **Zephaniah 3:9-13**

This loving conversion which Zephaniah prophesied is not just for Israel but for the nations. God will turn our speech from condemnation into praise and from confusing banter and language into a concatenation of worship.

We see here in Zephaniah that God will choose for Himself a people who are humble and meek who seek nothing but the name of Christ and His service. How beautiful to know that God will restore His people and that He has redeemed us not just for ourselves, but for the spread of His redemption. God has left for Himself a people to be marked by His character, humble, meek, justice seekers.

God will unite our speech for His glory. He is exalted through the rejoining of all peoples. What a beautiful foreshadowing of the Great Commission. We will be reunited in speech so that we can glorify the Father with one voice. Physical adoption is a taste of this reality on the lips of believers.

We see through physical adoption little boys and girls of different ethnicities, languages, skin tones, and tribes joined together under the banner of family. This is a brief snapshot of the reality of Heaven, the ultimate day when the nations will be reconciled.

Kai Christenberry was adopted by dear friends of ours Dr. Bill and Kim Christenberry. Kai is profoundly deaf and was born in China. When Kai came to saving faith in Christ he was baptized and gave this testimony: "I want to go back and share the gospel with the Chinese, especially the deaf who may never have another option to hear the good news." In June 2016, Kai had the opportunity to go back to China for the first time with a delegation from Lifeline to speak to 450 Chinese orphanage leaders.

Shortly thereafter, I was in China visiting a new opportunity in Huangzhou. The orphanage director was in the room when Kai spoke and was reminded of Lifeline by his testimony. She communicated to me that she wanted to work with Lifeline because of our Christian beliefs. She didn't completely understand what she was saying, but she saw the difference. She saw an organization committed to Christ and the people created in His image.

I pray that others will see in all of us that our call to care is not limited by ethnicity, skin color, or ability and that this will provide multiple opportunities to speak of the glorious gospel of Christ Jesus. When we lay down our lives at the cross of Christ, we will be led to invest in children like Kai from China and other nations so that they in turn can be a part of taking this gospel to all people groups.

Discussion Questions

1. In what ways are you blind to your own privilege? Or, in what ways have you been hurt by the blind privilege of others?

2. "Racism isn't a social issue. It's a family issue. May it be the same for the family of God." How has your church addressed this family issue? If it hasn't, how can you begin the conversation?

3. How does Psalm 139 plea with us to care for life both inside and outside of the womb?

4. Knowing Revelation 7:9-10 gives a multiethnic picture of heaven, how does that spur you on to pursue God's desire for His people now?

5. "We must despise and be as grieved about racism as we are about abortion, because the issues are the exact same. Both devalue a person made in God's image." How does this statement expand your view of "pro-life" to include racial reconciliation?

Chapter Five

RESPECTING WOMEN, HONORING MARRIAGE

Small in number, they were big in commitment. They were too God-intoxicated to be "intimidated." By their effort and example they brought an end to such ancient evils as infanticide and gladiator games. Things are different now... And if today's church does not recapture the sacrificial spirit of the early church, it will lose its authenticity, forfeit the loyalty of millions, and be dismissed as an irrelevant social club with no meaning for the twentieth century. Every day I meet young people whose disappointment with the church has turned into outright disgust.

— Dr. Martin Luther King, Jr., Letter from the Birmingham Jail

In 2016, Care Net, the largest network of pro-life pregnancy testing centers, conducted a study of women who had experienced an abortion. One shocking finding revealed that 33% of the women were attending church on a regular basis at the time of their first abortions. Even more astounding is that 70% identified as Christian at the time of their abortion.

Long before abortion came to be seen as a women's rights issue, the Church lost her heart in showing love to women. Our churches began programming everything to accommodate women and children, but simultaneously lost its voice in discipling men to cherish and love those same women.

Our children and families are reaping the consequences of this shift. The U.S. leads the world in no-contest divorces; Millennials are abandoning marriage as an institution; men are pleasing themselves selfishly by impregnating women and fleeing. Consequently, abortion is being used as birth control.

According to Care Net, 76% of women in a recent survey responded that the Church had no effect on their decision toward abortion. Furthermore, over half of participants believe that the Church oversimplifies decisions regarding pregnancy options, and they would not recommend someone experiencing an unexpected pregnancy go to a church for help. Nearly 66% of women agreed that the Church was more likely to gossip about a woman considering abortion rather than helping her navigate options.

When the Bride of Christ loses its influence to affect culture, marriages will crumble, children will struggle, and healthy families will dwindle. Instead of influencing culture toward the gospel, the Church has allowed the culture to be its shaping force. We no longer stand on our convictions and principles in the name of love and inclusion. Mercy and justice have been replaced by fussiness and politics. It's as Dr. Martin Luther King Jr. also said in his *Letter from the Birmingham Jail*,

> *There was a time when the church was very powerful. It was during that period that early Christians rejoiced when they were deemed worthy to suffer for what they believed. In those days the church was not merely a thermometer that recorded the ideas and principles of popular opinion; it was the thermostat that transformed the mores of society.*

In an effort to simplify our engagement, we as Christians have reduced our understanding of abortion to that of the murder of a child. We have castigated women in abortions as criminals. The truth is that women and children together are victims of abortion which is an all out affront to God and His holy institution: the family.

Beloved, in order to have a correct view of the sanctity of life, we need a correct understanding of what marriage means and what it looks like for women to be loved, led, and cared for in the name of Jesus.

Marriage is Crumbling for Convenience

In 2008, the divorce rate was reported to be 45% in the U.S.; however, the rate declined to 30% by 2018. While on the surface this may seem like a positive trend, it is important to note that the marriage rate over that same period decreased by almost 10%. Divorces are declining not because of a moral revolution, but as a result of fewer Americans entering into marriage, with the Millennial generation leading the way in delaying or forgoing marriage. They are the byproduct of former generations who mocked and destroyed the institution of marriage. Millennials, more than any other generation, have been born to single women, have experienced the divorce of their parents, and have seen fathers addicted to their work and hobbies.

A 2014 *Time Magazine* article entitled "The Beta Marriage: How Millennials Approach 'I Do'" found that marriage as an institution frightens Millennials. "Millennials aren't scared of commitment, they are just trying to do commitment more wisely....(they) are indeed trying to avoid failure."

Millennials are not only delaying marriage, but are also more likely to practice cohabitation and avoid monogamy. The article explains, "We're cynical. We are a generation raised on a wedding industry that could fund a small nation, but marriages that end before the ink has dried. (As one 29-year-old survey respondent put it: 'We don't trust that institution.') We are also less religious than any other generation, meaning we don't enter (or stay) committed simply for God. We feel less bound to tradition as a whole."

A 2009 article in *The New York Post* titled "The Five Year Marriage" reported that many nations are forgoing the marriage contracts which state until death do us part. In the article, Australian academic Helen Goltz proposed a shortening of marriage contracts with the argument that,

> We have fixed term-contracts for the buying of property, cars and insurance, but there is only one contract avai able for marriage and it is for life. Is it time to consider introducing fixed-term marriage contracts?"

Goltz continued that she believes that "life" is an unrealistic goal that puts undue pressure on a marriage. She said, "Instead, an expiration date puts the focus on making recommitments instead of the emotional turmoil of deciding to tear a union apart."

Time Magazine reported that Millennials agree with Goltz. According to a survey, given the option, more than 70% of Millennials would choose a fewer-than-10-year marriage contract, stating it would give them the option to leave. Only 20% of those surveyed chose to leave marriage contracts as lifetime commitments. The remainder of the respondents voted for polygamy.

Our culture's redefinition of marriage is a huge crisis, and whether we see it or not, women and children are the most vulnerable. Marriage was first made legal in our culture for the protection of children. Marriage helps in giving stability, belonging, and legal standing to a child. Contrary to prevailing thought, marriage also protects women. While it is not a popular trend in our current culture to notice any differences between men and women, the Bible certainly does. Pastor J.D. Greear, pastor of The Summit Church in Raleigh, North Carolina, says about the necessity of both genders,

> *God took the two genders and He divided up His attributes into the two genders so that the two of them together would be a better reflection of the Image of God than would one gender be by itself. God put part of Himself that man needs, that He is incomplete without, into the woman so that the two are necessary and they are interdependent. The two are not the same, if they were the same then one would be unnecessary.*

God's Word prescribes equal worth, but gives very different roles and responsibilities, which ultimately serve for protecting, nurturing, and leading of women.

A Marriage Built on the Gospel

Ephesians 5 contains the longest statement in the New Testament on marriage and the unique relationship between husbands and wives. While we see the foundations of marriage eroding in our culture, we see from God's Word that this began with the fall of man in Genesis 3. Jesus, however, came to redeem marriage, because it ultimately is a reflection and picture of the way that Christ relates to His Bride, the Church.

The question is simple: are we going to submit our marriages to the Word of God and to Christ or will we be shaped only by the culture?

Our God is a God of balance. He wants our lives to be lived for His glory. In order to be effective, He must reign supreme and our marriages, and families must take the next priority, so we can be well-balanced, healthy, and able to serve the Kingdom.

The Apostle Paul teaches about marriage in Ephesians 5:22-33, where he says,

> Wives, submit to your own husbands, as to the Lord. For the husband is the head of the wife even as Christ is the head of the Church, His body, and is Himself its Savior. Now as the Church submits to Christ, so also wives should submit in everything to their husbands.
>
> Husbands, love your wives, as Christ loved the Church and gave Himself up for her, that He might sanctify her, having cleansed her by the washing of water with the Word, so that He might present the Church to Himself in splendor, without spot or wrinkle or any such thing, that she might be holy and without blemish. In the same way husbands should love their wives as their own bodies. He who loves his wife loves himself. For no one ever hated his own flesh, but nourishes and cherishes it, just as Christ does the Church, because we are members of His body. "Therefore a man shall leave his father and mother and hold fast to his wife, and the two shall become one flesh." This mystery is profound, and I am saying that it refers to Christ and the Church. However, let each one of you love his wife as himself, and let the wife see that she respects her husband. —
> **Ephesians 5:22-23**

John Piper of Desiring God Ministries says, "Marriage is meant to be a living drama of how Christ and the Church relate to each other."

Marriage is a mystery of God and not a human invention. The glory of God is the ultimate aim of marriage. We see that everything in Ephesians 5 revolves around the glory of God. Marriage exists for God even more than it exists for husband and wife. When we honor marriage and the commitment required, we are honoring and glorifying God. In fact, we are showing the gospel and a correct picture of who God is when we have a biblical marriage. If we are worshipping our spouse or looking to our spouse for fulfillment before looking to the Lord, then we are going to end up dreadfully disappointed. I can try my best to love and cherish my wife Ashley; however, even on my best days I fall dreadfully short of supplying what she needs. She doesn't need an imperfect husband to supply her deepest longings. She needs Christ Jesus to meet her ultimate needs.

When two people submit completely to the Lord and enter into marriage looking not to be satisfied but to give out of the overflow of Christ, then marriage looks glorious. Beloved, we know that we are imperfect people who are prone to wander and sin, but if our starting point is seeking Christ, our marriage will grow in richness, tenderness, and reflect more of the glory of God. Glorifying Christ through our marriages is our aim. The supreme hope for our marriages is the grace of God. The God who ordained marriage is the One who gives the grace to sustain marriage, and we need abundant measures of grace daily in marriage.

We must take Romans 3:9-20 and apply it to marriage. In marriage we are bringing together a man and a woman whose *"'throats are open graves and tongues practice deceit. 'The poison of vipers is on their lips. 'Their mouths are full of cursing and bitterness. 'Ruin and misery mark their ways, and the way of peace they do not know. 'There is no fear of God before their eyes'"* (Rom. 3:13-18). When we enter marriage, we each bring our sinfulness with us. This is far from the picture that movies and television paint and is far from the mystique of dating. Marriage is the bringing together of two sinners for the glory of God. We need the gospel every day to empower us and to enable us. The gospel is the only hope for our marriage. It tells us who we are, but it shows us ultimately who Christ is and displays His grace for us. The truth is Christ is enough for your marriage.

For Ashley and me, our biggest disagreements are so simple, but show how complex our depravity is. My marriage needs Jesus and His grace and so does every marriage. The gospel is the ultimate picture of marriage. And this picture helps us see the different and unique roles of men and women while also proclaiming their equal worth.

When God created marriage in Genesis 2, He designed it to be a picture of the gospel where wives give a glimpse of the Church to the world, and husbands give a picture of Christ to the world. Wives are consistently giving a glimpse of the Church's submission and respect for Christ as she respects and submits to her husband. While men give a picture of the way that Christ nourishes, cherishes, and loves the world as he consistently loves and nourishes his wife.

Marriage is like a metaphor, an image, a picture, or parable that stands for something more than a man and a woman becoming one flesh. Marriage stands for the relationship between Christ and the Church. That's the deepest meaning of marriage. That brings tremendous responsibility for both the husband and wife to glorify God in their marriage.

Additionally, we see from Ephesians 5 that the husband is to lead his wife lovingly. He is the head of the marriage mirroring the way Christ relates to the church. Headship is not controlling, but lovingly serving. Headship is not an excuse to abuse, silence, or lord over a wife. Headship is not about worth or value. It is not a picture of inferiority or superiority. Galatians 3:28 affirms that we are all equal in Christ.

Headship is a picture of leadership and responsibility. Beloved, the simplest way to see this is to remember that Jesus stooped and washed His disciples' feet (the bridegroom, serving the bride), but not for one minute did any of the apostles in that room doubt who the leader was. The Bible would actually define headship as the divine calling of a husband to take primary responsibility for Christ-like servant leadership, protection, and provision in the home.

Husbands, as we read Ephesians 5, I hope we understand and see that the responsibility of marriage is harder on us than on our wives. The world sees these verses as chauvinistic and downgrading toward women, but in reality, the responsibility of servant-leadership is a gut check for men.

As husbands, it is our responsibility to love, care, protect and provide for our family. It is our responsibility as well to be unequivocally submitted to the Lordship of Christ, so that when our wives submit, they are ultimately submitting to Christ. Our wives don't need husbands who are the most successful in the culture's eye or who are the most macho. Our wives need husbands who are fully submitted to Christ, so in turn, as a husband, we will love and lead in a way that draws her closer to Christ. This reminds us that headship is not a right to command and control. It's a responsibility to love like Christ.

> *This reminds us that headship is not a right to command and control. It's a responsibility to love like Christ.*

Husbands, if we aren't careful, we can control and command our wives in an abusive way, and that is obviously not a reflection of Christ. Our attempts to control can be more subtle. We try to control and command her by trying to take the place of the Holy Spirit in her life. We can even become demeaning of her and harsh toward her sin struggles, but we must be reminded that headship is not a right to command and control, it's a responsibility to love like Christ.

The husband is to be like Christ, which means he is not Christ. The husband is finite in strength, not omnipotent like Christ. The husband is finite and fallible in wisdom, not all-wise like Christ. The husband is sinful, not perfect like Christ. Therefore, we husbands dare not assume we are infallible.

In the wife's submission to the headship of her husband, she is conforming ultimately to Christ, not her husband. The aim of the godly husband's leadership of his wife is to see her conformed to Christ, not controlled. Submission in marriage is to be mutual, but a husband's submission is to

Christ on his wife's behalf. The husband ultimately must be willing to die for his wife. This is radical, but also shows the true nature of a biblical marriage.

If a husband is loving and wise like Christ in all these ways, a humble wife will feel like she is being served, not humiliated. Headship is to reflect the love and character of Christ.

Headship also means that the husband is to sacrifice and love his wife while providing for her and protecting her. Without protection and provision, life itself is threatened. If a husband fails in his leadership here, there may not be any other place to exercise it. The life of the family hangs on protection and provision. Life itself must be protected and nourished, or it ceases to exist. Protection and provision have both a physical and a spiritual meaning. There is physical food that needs to be provided, as well as spiritual food that needs to be provided. Husbands need to protect against physical and spiritual threats to the life of the family.

John Piper, who served for several decades as a pastor, says,

> When a man senses a primary God-given responsibility for the spiritual life of the family, gathering the family for devotions, taking them to church, calling for prayer at meals — when he senses a primary God-given responsibility for the discipline and education of the children, the stewardship of money, the provision of food, the safety of the home, the healing of discord, that special sense of responsibility is not authoritarian or autocratic or domineering or bossy or oppressive or abusive. It is simply servant leadership. And I have never met a wife who is sorry she is married to a man like that. Because when God designs a thing (like marriage), He designs it for His glory and our good.

So brother, love your wife completely and unselfishly, nourish her, protect and provide for her, and be compassionate and tender with her heart. The way we love and lead our wives reflects Christ, and that's a high calling.

So, ladies, if men lead in this way, it can make submission a glad-hearted endeavor. Submission to this type of leadership values your worth instead of demeaning you. Through submission, the wife is to be the helper for her husband, mirroring the way the Church relates to Christ. Submission literally means to yield to one's loving leadership.

Christ subordinated Himself to the Father during His earthly ministry. He consistently submitted Himself to the will of the Father. Whatever the Father said, He did. When the Father told Him to speak, He spoke. This is not inferiority, inequality, or coercion. This is a voluntary submission, trusting, yielding and devotion to another person. It's a good thing. Revere Christ and out of that reverence, submit to your husband, because it is the divine calling of a wife to honor and affirm her husband's leadership and help carry it through according to her gifts.

The wife uses her gifts to assist her husband in his leadership. A husband needs to know he is significant to his wife, like he needs air. In the same way that a wife wants and craves love, the husband needs respect. But ladies, remember submission to your husband is not identical to your submission to Christ. Wives submit to a perfect God while honoring an imperfect husband.

There are so many examples that I could include of how my sweet wife Ashley supports me in our endeavor to serve Christ daily that if I listed them all it would take another volume. As I travel the world showing the love of Christ to orphans, she stays at home teaching, instructing, and discipling our children. While they desperately miss me and always ask why does daddy have to leave, she reminds them that they all are such an integral part of the ministry through their sacrifice.

When I am home, we desperately want to lead our family in worship and devotion. Ashley never doubts that this is my heart's desire, but she knows that many times my execution can be limited because of the busyness of life. She lovingly picks the best resources, finds the time when we are all together, and then sets me up for success in leading our children to love the Lord.

Brothers and sisters, this is a divine partnership where gifts are complementary. The Lord allows me to write and preach and has given me the ability to easily explain scripture. In the same way He has gifted my wife with the ability to edit, find pertinent examples, and encourage me in the proclamation. She helps me, honors me, and complements me. All of our ultimate submission must be to Christ and, wives, as you submit totally to Christ, you will find it easier to honor your imperfect husband because you will begin to love him as Christ loves him.

A wife will see the need for change in her husband because he is imperfect, and it's hard to submit and honor a sinner. The wife should seek the transformation of her husband, even while respecting him as her head— her leader, protector, and provider. Wives, pray daily that your husbands would be conformed to the image of Christ. My sweet wife, Ashley, is my prayer warrior, and I am confident that she is praying for me and my needs, but also that I may look more like Christ.

Additionally, wives, be a consistently loving sister in Christ to your husband. Wives are not only wives, but in Christ, you are also loving sisters. There is a unique way for a submissive wife to be a caring sister toward her imperfect brother/husband. As a sister and co-heir in Christ, lovingly guard the witness of your husband and lovingly confront him in his sin for the glory of God and the gospel. Peter talks about this kind of sacrificial, loving response on behalf of an unbelieving husband in 1 Peter 3:1-6. He encourages wives to put on Christlike character within as an act of worship to God and an act of love to lead their husbands toward Jesus.

I also acknowledge that many women find themselves married to unbelievers. Either they came to Christ after marriage or they learned that their husband was only masquerading as a Christian. I would exhort these wives to respect their husbands and give deference to them as much as they can, while praying for their salvation; however, never give deference to a husband, unbelieving, wayward, or even Christian husband when his leadership is in direct opposition to the Word of God and to the gospel of Christ. Even in your disagreement, live at peace, so that you do not become a stumbling block to the work of the Spirit. Wives, the way you honor an unbelieving husband or a wayward husband can be used by God to show such a sweet reflection of the grace of God. When you show respect to a husband who is doing nothing to earn it, you are giving the Holy Spirit ample ground to use your honor as an avenue to your husband's heart.

Also, let me be clear. The call for submission by wives is not to be interpreted as a call to endure abuse, ever. Marriage was meant to protect and provide for God's image bearers, especially women and children. Christ would never abuse His Church nor allow her to be abused. Men, we must always protect our wives from abuse as well as single women and battered wives.

The family is God's institution for human flourishing. When we operate in loving harmony with a husband nourishing his wife through leadership and a wife respecting her husband in deference to Christ, we are showing the world that we are truly pro-life. When we have healthy, God-fearing families, we begin to see a picture of health which will show justice of the Kingdom of God to the world. Our healthy families create confident children and strong churches.

Beloved, don't miss that being pro-life means being pro-woman, pro-marriage, and pro-family. May our marriages and families begin to reflect the Lord in such a way that single pregnant women can see the love of the Kingdom displayed in a way that gives her hope for the life inside her womb.

Planned Parenthood, Ashley Madison and the Gospel

The summer of 2015 brought a flurry of activity in the U.S. which gave two very heart-wrenching commentaries on our culture.

Planned Parenthood made headlines in videos, released by The Center for Medical Progress, detailing the grotesque realities of harvesting unborn babies for research and stem cells. These videos exposed the moral depravity of our world as babies, made in the image of God, are reduced to a choice and an economic commodity. What had been knit together with care in their mothers' wombs is plundered amid hearty laughs and jokes.

However, these videos didn't just indict the secular; it ultimately showed how stagnant and apathetic the Bride of Christ has become. We, the Church, cried out in outrage at these videos but how soon we forgot that this holocaust on human life had been legally protected since 1973. We cried out; we tweeted; we fussed; we protested; we posted on social media; and we even called out Planned Parenthood within our hateful statements.

But, ultimately we were inactive.

> I know your works: you are neither cold nor hot. Would that you were either cold or hot! So, because you are lukewarm, and neither hot nor cold, I will spit you out of My mouth. —**Revelation 3:15-16**

> So also faith by itself, if it does not have works, is dead. —**James 2:17**

Church, we have become impotent and lethargic. Our words are cutting and strong, but our actions are weak and feeble. We are pro-birth, but we have failed to be pro-life. We have categorized the women who are preyed on by Planned Parenthood as villains instead of victims — victims both of self and sin. They don't need our condemning words or our rhetoric; they need our Savior, and they need our presence.

Instead of being present and mentoring women and men in crisis; instead of opening up our homes to help, even when adoption may not be an option; instead of modeling our marriages and our homes to a world that needs gospel-saturated families and marriages, we prostitute ourselves like Gomer (Hosea's wife) and indulge secretly in the pleasures of the world. Our indifference and lethargy does nothing more than fuel hurt, pain, violence, and abandonment of children.

And the headlines and statistics during the summer of 2015 proved that the men of the Church are more interested in pornography and affairs than loving their wives. Shortly after the Planned Parenthood videos were released, a group called The Impact Team revealed the database of names engaged with an online site, Ashley Madison, which would arrange affairs.

Ann Voskamp wrote in a blog, *"You know they're laughing at us, right?"* *She said,*

> They're laughing at us because we make the gospel a comedy with our hypocrisy, and our lack of monogamy, and our puffed up religiosity and dishonesty and our self-righteous animosity. They're laughing at us because we trivialize the gospel because we monetize it, because we cheapen it and we sell it, because we make ourselves comfortable with it—instead of dying for it.

Brothers, we are called to love our wives like Christ loves the Church. That means loving this precious, image-bearer of God even when the dailiness of life seems boring, even when her sin makes her unlovable, even when she wounds our ego, even when she fails to respect our leadership or rebels against our love. 'Til death do us part. We do this because our marriages are a picture of the gospel. This is a picture that the world needs more than our rhetoric. Our wives and our children need our presence and our dependence on God.

So brothers, put down the smartphone and pick up a Bible. Stop looking at porn; stop fueling human trafficking; and stop throwing stones at Planned Parenthood while your actions on Ashley Madison's website and others keeps them in business. Life is short. Pray more. Cling to the Word. Love your wife. Pray for God's grace to fight temptation and to escape it. *"No temptation has overtaken you that is not common to man. God is faithful, and he will not let you be tempted beyond your ability, but with the temptation he will also provide the way of escape, that you may be able to endure."* 1 Corinthians 10:13.

We don't need the U.S. government to defund Planned Parenthood. We need our hearts changed and our deeds altered so that our lives defund Planned Parenthood.

Church, what would happen if we got to know the family next door? What would happen if we stopped running our kids to endless activities and freed our schedules to get involved in the lives of pregnant women, foster children and their families, and orphans and their families?

Stop wasting your life on Facebook and social media and invest your life in gospel transformation and discipleship.

What if tomorrow the U.S. Supreme Court made abortion illegal? Are we really ready for that? Are our churches ready to not only promote birth, but to help women raise their children for life? Will we be willing and ready to stand in the gap? Will we open our homes to adoption and foster care? Will we use our time to be mentors and disciple makers?

Beloved, are we really willing to let the gospel reclaim our families?

May the gospel restore our homes! May our lives not be wasted but be spent for the gospel! And may the gospel displayed in our lives show the mercy and grace of our Lord Jesus, that while we were still sinners, Christ came and became our sacrifice.

Gomer was a prostitute but the Lord called Hosea, her husband, to pursue her with unending love and unlimited grace. This pursuit is a picture of what the Lord does for us. May the words of Hosea 11:10 ring true:

> They shall go after the Lord; He will roar like a lion; when He roars, His children shall come trembling from the west; they shall come trembling like birds from Egypt, and like doves from the land of Assyria, and I will return them to their homes, declares the Lord.

Beloved, are you ready to stand in the gap and love and lead the women around you?

Discussion Questions

1. What is your reaction to the statistics and stories shared in this chapter regarding our culture's redefinition of marriage? How is this the antithesis of God's design for marriage to reflect Christ and the Church?

2. How does applying Romans 3:9-20 to marriage help us see our sin and live in the truth that only Christ can sustain marriage? How does that give you compassion for unbelievers in marriage?

3. Using Ephesians 5:22-33, how are you fulfilling your role as a husband or wife? If not married, how does this scripture inform your evaluation of a potential spouse and help you grasp the picture of Biblical marriage as opposed to cultural marriage?

4. Through what practical ways can you advocate for being pro-life by expanding that definition to include being pro-woman, pro-marriage, and pro-family?

Chapter Six

FATHERLESSNESS

Train boys to be men. Dads, husbands, and single men, show boys what
godly responsibility, humble initiative, and hard-working leadership looks
like in action. Train boys to provide, protect, and to lead women in loving,
gracious, humble, and hard-working ways that reflect the very character
of Christ. Show them that this is what the cross compels us to do.

— Dr. David Platt, Pastor McLean Bible Church

On February 14, 2018, a 19-year-old young man named Nikolas Cruz opened gun fire with an AR-15 at about 2:18 P.M. Eastern Standard Time in Parkland, Florida, at Marjory Stoneman Douglas High School. That Wednesday, Cruz killed 17 people and wounded many others while leaving an otherwise sleepy community in devastated shock.

The *New York Times* released an article February 15, 2018, by Richard Faussett and Serge Kovaleski, claiming Cruz demonstrated "red flags" that should have alerted others to pay closer attention to his behavior. The "red flags" included the following:

- Diagnoses of depression, ADHD, and autism
- Adopted at a young age, along with his brother, by older parents (48 & 61)
- Witnessing his dad's death by a heart attack at the age of 5
- Mom's death in November 2017
- Being ostracized by classmates and becoming a reject
- Expulsion from Stoneman Douglas High School for assaulting another student

In the aftermath of a tragedy like this, we have questions and want to see these types of things stopped. Governor Rick Scott went as far as to promise to "do everything he can to make sure this never happens again." In 2017, our country averaged more than one school shooting each week. What's the answer to this crisis? What can we do? What should we do? What is our response to situations like this from a Christian worldview?

The prophet Jeremiah quotes the Lord in Chapter 17: Thus says the Lord: *'Cursed is the man who trusts in man and makes flesh his strength, whose heart turns away from the Lord.'"* According to Jeremiah, gun control alone will not stop violence. As a matter of fact, we are cursed if we trust in the laws of man to solve this dilemma. We cannot solve school shootings with laws or social policies. Our politics cannot stop violence and hurt or even begin to heal our land. Neither man nor the systems created by man can really heal pain. Rightly, Jeremiah says in verse 6 that the one who trusts in the flesh, *"is like a shrub in the desert, and shall not see any good come. He shall dwell in the parched places of the wilderness, in an uninhabited salt land."*

This is our current culture — parched and in the wilderness. We have immense prosperity, riches, assets, and weaponry, but we have forsaken the Lord. We have racial discord, violence, thievery, selfishness, anger, divorce, and abortion. Jeremiah 17:9 reminds us that, *"the heart is deceitful above all things, and desperately sick; who can understand it?"*

These truths should not lead us to be fatalistic because Jeremiah reminds us in 17:7-8: *"Blessed is the man … whose trust is the Lord. He is like a tree planted by water … and does not fear when heat comes … and is not anxious in the year of drought, for it does not cease to bear fruit."* As God's people, we must trust fully in God and do what He says if we want to see healing in our land.

One of the saddest lines from *The New York Times* article about Cruz reports, "Mr. Gold, a neighbor, said that Mr. Cruz at one point had gone to a school for students with special needs. 'Kids were really picking on him and would gang up on him and beat him up a little,' Mr. Gold said. 'They ostracized him. He didn't have many friends.'"

The Bible teaches that man is accountable for his own actions; however, I wonder what would have happened if the Church had reached out and shown love, care, and concern to that boy. What could have happened if the gospel of grace would have been displayed? I am not absolving Cruz of evil, and he must stand trial for his wrong doings both in a court of law and in the court of Heaven. The question is, though, what might have happened if a local church had taken an active role to help his mother Lynda, a widow taking care of two boys? What would have happened if the church had supported and held up this struggling family by pointing them to the grace of Jesus? What could the outcome have been if Cruz had known the life-giving hope found only in Jesus?

Beloved, we are called to care for orphans and widows, not because it is easy, comfortable, or convenient, but because when we display the gospel of the Lord Jesus Christ to the vulnerable, the gospel itself begins to take root and change their lives.

Again, I am not absolving Cruz of fault or ascribing it to anyone in his life who tried to care for him, but I want us, as believers, to dig deep and ask ourselves what can we do to manifest the gospel to our neighbors, the poor, the orphan and widow? Do you know a child in crisis like Cruz? Do you know a family on the verge of crisis?

When we stand in the gap for children and families, we just might be keeping another child off the streets and out of trouble. When we disciple and equip vulnerable children overseas either through adoption or orphan care we might be training up the next leader who makes the gospel known to the nations.

Caring for vulnerable children and families will cost us our comfort, our ease, and potentially our reputation, but this is the call of the gospel found in James 1:27. The call is to reach into the distress and the messy to those who have been ostracized because they have no one to stand up for them. God is asking us to stand up for them and to put our lives in action to bring them hope.

Isaiah speaks of this hope:

> *The Spirit of the Lord God is upon me, because the Lord has anointed me to bring good news to the poor; He has sent me to bind up the brokenhearted, to proclaim liberty to the captives, and the opening of the prison to those who are bound; to proclaim the year of the Lord's favor, and the day of vengeance of our God; to comfort all who mourn; to grant to those who mourn in Zion — to give them a beautiful headdress instead of ashes, the oil of gladness instead of mourning, the garment of praise instead of a faint spirit; that they may be called oaks of righteousness, the planting of the LORD, that he may be glorified.* — **Isaiah 61:1-3**

I have learned something in my travels to China that illustrates how I think about putting this passage into action. The Chinese character for "crisis" is part of the character set that makes up the Chinese words for "danger" and "opportunity." That may seem perplexing and counterintuitive, but I believe it is profound.

We have an orphan crisis in our country and in our world. We have a problem in the U.S. of pervasive fatherlessness that is chronic and dangerous; over 50% of American children born this year will be born to single women. Beloved, this is a crisis!

More specifically, it is a crisis involving men and boys. CNN compiled a list of the deadliest shootings in U.S. history, noting that all the shooters were men, except for one instance involving a husband and a wife. Just after the Cruz incident, *Fox News* released an article declaring, "Boys are broken." The article documents a common thread between most mass murderers; they are fatherless. Warren Farrell, author of *The Boy Crisis*, said after a 2013 shooting,

> *We blame guns, violence in the media, violence in video games, and poor family values. Each is a plausible player, but our daughters live in the same homes, with the same access to the same guns, video games and media and are raised with the same family values. Our daughters are not killing. Our sons are.*

The reason "boys are broken" is deeper than policy changes, politics, National Rifle Association (NRA) lobbying, or even what our government can fix. How many more innocent children will have to die before we look at the root cause of brokenness in these boys?

Boys have lost their identity. Boys were meant to be image bearers of the Creator as they show the strength, character, and stability of our great God. Men are lost wasting their time on video games, smart phones, and digital infidelity and adultery.

According to the Entertainment Software Association (ESA), nearly $91.5 billion was spent on video games and gaming products around the globe in 2015, with the U.S. accounting for nearly a quarter of that ($22 billion). Gaming has become as popular as pet ownership. Two-thirds of Americans say they play video games daily stating they play on average more than three hours a week. Reportedly men are more than three times as likely to indulge in video games.

We are truly *Amusing Ourselves to Death*, as Neil Postman so aptly entitled his 1985 book. And all of this amusement while according to census data from 2017, one in three children in America grow up in homes without the influence of a father. That's nearly 24 million children in America without fathers. There is a crisis in America.

According to the National Fatherhood Initiative, research shows that when a child is raised in a father-absent home, he or she is affected in the following ways:

- Children are more than 10 times as likely to experience neglect and abuse.
- Girls are seven times more likely to become pregnant as a teenager.
- Children are at a four times greater risk for poverty.
- Children are two times more likely to suffer from obesity.
- Students are two times more likely to drop out of high school.
- Children are more likely to abuse substances and to suffer emotional and behavioral problems.

In addition:

- In U.S. prisons, 92% of incarcerated parents are fathers.
- Of incarcerated fathers, only 20% grew up in a home with their father.

These statistics are staggering and remind us that the battle for life and the pro-life agenda must extend past anti-abortion laws and pregnancy resource centers and into the hearts and homes of our children. Children need godly men in their lives, even if their father is unavailable.

I can think of no greater example of what this looks like in practical action than what I have seen my Ugandan brother, Pastor Raphael Kajjubi, continuously do for the last ten years in a village outside of Kampala, Uganda, called Busega. Raphael is the pastor of King Jesus Church, which he planted in the heart of this predominately Muslim area.

Raphael was previously leading a large church with his brother in Kampala. This larger church was attached to Western funders and was venturing into prosperity theology. Raphael and his wife Allen had everything that a Ugandan could dream of—a nice home, school fees for their daughters, and earthly security. However, the Holy Spirit created great unrest in the heart of the Kajjubi family as they saw Muslim boys rejected by their fathers, vulnerable children roam the streets, and Muslims take over the slum of Busega. He begins,

> Two years before we started King Jesus Church we sensed a need to move into the community, so we rented a small apartment which was part of three attached houses. The man in the middle had lived and worked in Europe for many years and he used most of the money which he had accumulated to attract young people. They would line up at his door and beg for something to eat and for attention. He took advantage of these children's vulnerability and did much ugliness and many unspeakable things to these innocent souls.

However, God has a unique way to use tragedy to reveal Himself. Because of where our family was positioned, we were able to begin ministering to the victims, sharing the love of Christ, and disciplining them to health. Many of these same victims serve with us today on our ministry team at King Jesus.

When I look back ten years ago when this was going on, what we did was simple. We invited these kids in our small house, prayed with them and studied truths of Scriptures with them. As many opened their lives to the saving grace and knowledge of Jesus Christ, they began to realize their lives were much more than just a piece of bread. After they had encountered the real radical love and grace of Christ, they were transformed into the major agents of God's grace and hope that they are today.

From the radical obedience of my brother Raphael to move his family from prosperity to relative obscurity, the small fellowship of believers in their humble apartment outgrew the space and forced them to move into a theater which showed "dirty movies, housed strippers, and contained a bar." However, through consistency in the proclamation of the Word and investment into the lives of young men, the church saw more young men come to saving faith and to serve alongside King Jesus Church.

Then in 2010, Raphael and I met and he told me, "We were introduced to about five deaf children who were treated less than animals in their own families or on the street." Now, nine years later, Raphael says:

As a result of our partnership with Lifeline these deaf kids, and now their Muslim families, have been greatly affected. We began having these kids come to the church to learn sign language and expose them to the gospel. Today several serve on our ministry team and are such an integrated part of our faith family. Yet the beauty and joy in all this is that friends, neighbors and the whole community see a loving and understanding expression of the gospel from a thriving church in the center of their community. To the praise and glory of God, now 25 'formerly worthless' children are having a daily opportunity to experience school, a church community and opportunities for work and social advancement.

Through this work, we have received the attention of other churches and as a result, a network of pastors and Christian leaders has developed into The Greater Busega Area Pastors Fellowship. We meet on a weekly basis for at least two hours to pray together, share the Word together and discuss struggles. In the beginning, the infiltration of the prosperity gospel was so strong among the group, but we are seeing these pastors and leaders begin to embrace sound theology and exposition of what the gospel truly is!

As I have travelled to Uganda many times and Busega specifically, the Lord has given me the opportunity to preach at King Jesus Church, to help disciple their leadership teams, and to host a pastors' training for the Busega network. The resounding question has been, "where are the older men?" Muslim groups from Libya specifically targeted this community because of the over abundance of young fatherless men and women. They believed if they could educate these young people in new schools, they could reprogram their world and life view.

While the Muslims were targeting the community, Westerners were importing the prosperity gospel to the poor and needy within an impoverished area. The outcome was weak and shallow faith which gave way to a complete ideology change within a short ten years. Busega, once a strong bastion for Christ, is now a clearly majority Muslim stronghold within the Christian nation of Uganda. Then sadly, once the Muslims took over, the remaining Christians left.

Raphael has continually told me that this sad reality has left an already struggling village in even greater despair. But my brother also proclaims that as followers of King Jesus, we must not cower back in fear, but boldly approach the throne of grace and go into the hardest to reach areas with the light of the gospel. I'll let him share his heart in his own words:

When we first started, we realized the problems that affected the unbelievable levels of poverty around Busega were really deeper than just people not having food, clothes and the other many physical needs of people all over the world, but the lack of fathers or at least the lack of active fathers. Sin, which had grown and produced such evil that you cannot imagine or even give description to, had invaded the hearts and minds of the older men that they rejected their families and rejected our message. But the young people received us because we were present and available. So we began investing in them, discipling them, and training them. Today we see mature young men who have started their own families, are working responsibly, and are leading in the church and their community. The good news is that now some of the older men and women are finally beginning to respond to the message of the gospel!

The Church is and shall always be God's means to reach and reconcile hostile people back to God. The Church, even with all of her inadequacies, is used by God to bring people together, connect them to Jesus and to each other. All that we have done is to be available, to preach the gospel, and to provide a place of belonging called the "Church."

The true preaching of God's Word has been such a key instrument in its infallible work of convicting hearts and bringing repentance. One such example is that of James, who serves on our leadership team. He previously refused to speak before more than three people because he claimed he was shy and reserved. As he continued to participate in our Bible studies and prayer meetings he realized that part of the Christian privilege is to be a witness of our Savior and Lord Jesus. Today, he joyfully shares and boldly leads hundreds of people. Again, all we have done is to continue to proclaim faithfully and teach the Word of God.

The secret cost of discipleship is trusting and then building fellowship among sinful and unlovable people. With all these groups of people God has placed us among, I must confess it has been hard and painful. Recently, we woke up to the news of the death by stoning of one of our deaf children at the school. A gang in the community mistook him for a thief, simply because he could not speak. This was a dark day, but the beauty came when one turned to Christ and their life changed. When we see the Lord snatch these image bearers from "death" to "life," we realize that it is worth all of our sacrifice.

So we keep working and trusting that the God who changed us shall do it again and again in the life of His people whom He has placed us among. The gospel and its power is what changes life, not human efforts. We aren't seeking social transformation, but gospel proclamation which transforms the hearts and lives of the community. It's now been over ten years, and we have seen many lives snatched from the power of darkness to this marvelous hope found in Christ Jesus. It has been worth it all — especially when we see those whom the Lord allowed us to invest in, invest in others.

Beloved, no matter the context, country, culture, or calling, the fatherless need our availability, our proclamation of the gospel, our consistency, and discipleship. Men of God, we must embrace the gospel, get in the game, and wrap our lives around the boys in our home and in our community by pointing them to the gospel. We need to introduce young men to the Father that fights for His children by laying down His own life.

It is easy to see the danger in this crisis, but do we see the opportunity? Have we rejoiced in the opportunity? Have we seized the opportunity? Our God is inviting us into these places to care for the orphan and the widow, and ultimately to see the gospel change their reality and story.

As the Chinese character reminds us, there is no opportunity without crisis and impending danger. So the question is, will you seize the opportunity that the Lord has placed at your feet to faithfully follow Christ Jesus into the dangerous, perilous, and messy world of caring for children with a distinctive pro-life ministry?

Will you seize the opportunity to show hope and love to the Nikolas Cruz in your life, so that the gospel can change him before he makes tomorrow's headlines? Seizing this opportunity will take work. Fatherless children are probably not going to come and find you. You will need to be proactive in engaging them by volunteering at school, in community programs, and in your church.

Practical steps for investing in the fatherless around you:

1. Show the grace and love of God as a family to mothers. It is important to remember that moms bear the burden when dads are missing, disconnected, or absent. As a family we must support these moms and then ask for their permission to invest in her children.

2. Pray for the fatherless at home and out loud. Simply ask these children and their families how you can pray for them and then do it. Every night before my kids go to bed and I am home, I pray over them. There is a good chance that many children have never experienced someone praying specifically for them to their Creator.

3. Invest time by having fun with the fatherless through activities they enjoy. My son, Caleb, and I invested recently in the lives of some neighborhood kids by playing basketball with them. While playing ball, it gave us immense opportunities to encourage them, speak truth, and to probe their hearts.

4. Build relationships with fatherless children through volunteering at their school or coaching a community sports team. Use these opportunities to open the Word of God, read it with them, and help them learn how to study it. The Word of God is living and active and it holds the true words of life, hope, and healing.

5. Get the fatherless engaged with the local church. First, you are the local church, but we must get the fatherless engaged in the larger community of faith so that they can create strong, vibrant, and encouraging relationships.

Discussion Questions

1. Our world is broken and daunting, and caring for the vulnerable will cost us our comfort and ease. How are you encouraged by Isaiah 61:1-3 when considering this?

2. How do we see opportunity in crisis? How do we encourage each other to rejoice in and seize that opportunity?

3. Knowing that fatherless children will most likely not come to find you, how can you practically be proactive in finding and engaging with them?

4. We know that those whom the Lord allows us to invest in may invest in others. Considering this, what might be the impact of us neglecting to invest in gospel relationships with the fatherless?

Chapter Seven

GODLY MEN =
STRONG FATHERS

Older men are to be sober-minded, dignified, self-controlled, sound
in faith, in love, and in steadfastness.... Likewise, urge the younger men
to be self-controlled. Show yourself in all respects to be a model of
good works, and in your teaching show integrity, dignity, and sound
speech that cannot be condemned, so that an opponent may be
put to shame, having nothing evil to say about us.

— Titus 2:2, 6-8

On May 1, 2003, I walked into the office of the Senior Auditing Partner at Warren, Averett, Kimbrough, and Marino, LLC, where I was working as a Senior Accountant, to announce that I had accepted a new role as the Executive Director of Lifeline Children's Services, Inc.

He looked at me befuddled and perplexed. Joe was a prankster, and he knew I loved humor too. So, thinking this was just a joke, he looked at me and announced, "Moses (my middle name)! Go back to your office. You are on the fast track to big things around here. That's not funny."

He then looked into my face, and I think realized this was no joke. I was the office "good Christian," and he knew I was serious. Trying to reason with me for real this time, "Moses, seriously, you don't need to throw away your promising career on a women's ministry. Doesn't Ashley already do that kind of work?"

He was right. My wife Ashley was the Assistant Director of a local pregnancy center, Sav-A-Life. He knew our passion. He even knew our commitment, yet he did not understand.

Expecting to be excused that day from my employment (two weeks notices were rarely needed at such a large firm) and to start immediately at Lifeline, Joe tried his last ditch effort. "Moses, you are giving me at least a two-weeks notice, right? Give me until Monday, May 19 at noon, and you are free to come to your senses."

The stories are too numerous to tell of all the perplexed conversations that followed my encounter with Joe. Why would a male accountant with a Master's degree work in a "women's ministry"?

I had always perplexed my colleagues, but before it had always been because they said I lived out what I believed. I would not ride in the car or eat with a woman alone. I would not go out after work drinking or to the strip club. I did not curse nor did I say anything negative about my wife as much as they tried to encourage me. I loved my time at WAKM, and I genuinely loved the people I worked with and for, but the Lord had placed a new call upon my life. This call did not make sense to my co-workers, and quite frankly, it was radical and weird even for the "good Christian."

Before you dismiss this as a misunderstanding with the secular world, I would like you to consider one thing, the truth is that even in the Church, pro-life issues and championing the sanctity of life have become a "woman's issue." Too often I hear, even in adoption and foster care ministries, that men are active only because "my wife got us into this." Before this was a woman's issue, God first ordained the man to be the defender of life.

In a culture that undermines the traditional family, minimizes the roles of fathers, and rejects the marks of the Maker, we must celebrate the fact that daddies matter to families equally in the way mommies matter. God designed men and women uniquely to play specific roles in the family unit. When those roles are thwarted, broken, or dismissed, weak families and a confused society are the results.

My friend Rick Burgess, host of the nationally syndicated radio program "The Rick and Bubba Show" and co-author of the book *How to Be a Man*, says, "Let's teach our men how to be the spiritual leaders of their homes. If you take the men of the Church from spiritual infancy to spiritual maturity you will solve a lot of problems in the Church and in our world today."

Burgess and his co-author, Andy Blanks, further conclude in their book,

> *Examples of what a real man is can be hard to come by. The big problem is simply that you're starving for good examples of what a man is. Some of you don't know exactly where to look for your model. Some of you look around and what you see gives you mixed messages. Is your model the over-the-top, super competitive, hyper-masculine guy who never met a challenge, or a person, he couldn't conquer? Or is your model the 20-something who has "failed to launch" and spends his days sleeping and his nights playing video games in his parents' basement? Is your model the workaholic adult in your life? Or is your model the gender-neutral guy who thinks all of this masculinity talk is kind of crazy? Even the godliest guy you know isn't a perfect example. ... Through His life, death, and resurrection, Jesus makes it possible for you to have an identity that is completely found in Himself.*

Many of the birth mothers we work with at Lifeline come to us with huge "daddy wounds." These wounds are either inflicted by a father who was absent, abusive, or apathetic. My wife saw this consistently in her work at the pregnancy resource center. When Ashley would counsel women seeking abortion, the predominant excuses were either "my dad would kill me" or "my dad hasn't been around for years."

Remember the *New York Post* article I referred to in Chapter 5 proposing short-term marriage contracts? Well, in all honesty, we really aren't too far it in practice. According to 2018 census data, the average marriage in the U.S. lasts 8.2 years and just under 50% of all marriages will end in divorce (this includes all marriages, even multiple marriages, not just first marriages). Sadly, Goltz was simply proposing something to try to absolve guilt from an already present reality by noting that "an expiration date puts the focus on making recommitments instead of the emotional turmoil of deciding to tear a union apart. If the husband and wife decide not to re-up, the union would simply dissolve, without the 'shame and stigma' associated with divorce."

Beloved, this is upside down and the result of when sinful men try to rearrange the natural order and creation of man. God simply says it in Genesis 2:24, *"Therefore a man shall leave his father and his mother and hold fast to his wife, and they shall become one flesh."* Since the fall, sin and Satan have attacked and utterly conquered families and in particular, men. We live today in a culture where it is almost accursed to be masculine.

It should be no surprise that we live in such a society. Traditional families have an enemy, and it isn't the LGBTQ agenda, government, tolerance, or Hollywood. The enemy is the same enemy introduced in Genesis 3. The enemy is the great serpent Satan. From the beginning of Creation, Satan has warred against God's design. He has been bent toward destruction and absolute decimation of everything that God had called "good" in creation.

We can't overlook God's design for family during the temptation of Genesis 3. God made man and woman as complementary. He gave the man the role of the leader and woman the role of the helper. Woman was made for man because he was incomplete without her. It was man's role to love the woman, protect her, and point her to the Father.

God's first commands were given to man before woman was even created. His single prohibition was contained in these commands in Genesis 2:17, *"but of the tree of the knowledge of good and evil you shall not eat, for in the day that you eat of it you shall surely die."*

The very next thing out of God's mouth in verse 18 was, *"It is not good that the man should be alone; I will make him a helper fit for him."* It was the man's job to lead the woman and to guard her heart. It was his job to help her understand the goodness of God and His great love and ultimate protection.

The first sin was aided by the apathy of the man. Satan was already working to bring enmity in God's perfect relationship. He was tempting the man toward being weak and apathetic while tempting the woman to take on the role of the leader.

When Genesis 3 begins with this first temptation and the fall of man, make no mistake, while the attack was supremely against the relationship between God and His creation, it was an attack on the horizontal family as well.

> *So when the woman saw that the tree was good for food, and that it was a delight to the eyes, and that the tree was to be desired to make one wise, she took of its fruit and ate, and she also gave some to her husband who was with her, and he ate.* —**Genesis 3:6**

And so the war on the traditional family began; followed by murder, polygamy, incest, fornication, homosexuality, men abusing their wives, prostitution, abortion, and no-contest divorce.

This is why, men of God, we need to seek God with all of our hearts, with all of our minds, and with all of our souls and to love our wives as we love ourselves. We need to take up the weapons of this war and fight back for the sake of our marriages, for the sake of our families, and for the sake of the gospel to the nations.

Our great God calls Himself our Father. He compares Himself to the groom seeking after his bride (the Church) and as the Father who pursues his prodigal son. Men, we are image bearers of the godly pursuit. Our wives are craving our leadership and our role is vital to our children.

Dr. David Platt says,

> *God created men and women with equal dignity, both men and women created in the image of God, in the likeness of God, as representatives of God. Man not superior to woman; woman not superior to man. Any man who belittles a woman is violating the design of God. Any woman who disparages a man is undercutting the beautiful design of God. Men and women created by God with equal dignity. At the same time, created with different roles, roles that don't call into question one's dignity or worth in any way.*
>
> *He created men and women as a reflection of the Trinity. God the Father, God the Son, God the Spirit. Equal in essence, worth; different in role. It's not chauvinistic or domineering for God the Father to have authority over God the Son; for God the Son to submit to God the Father. For the Son to sit at the right hand of the Father is not a bad thing. This is a good thing. This is where we see that understanding the personhood of God is huge for understanding our own manhood and womanhood. Created, all of us, men and women, with equal dignity, different roles, for our good and His glory.*

The New York Times published an article on a study from the *Journal of Developmental Psychology*, May 2017, called, "The Link Between Detached Dads and Risk-Taking Girls." Melvin Conner summarized the report, "It's all about the exposure to dads; the bigger the dose, the more fathering matters — for better or for worse. ... The prolonged presence of a warm and engaged father can buffer girls against early, high-risk sex."

So as my friend, Karyn Purvis, author of *The Connected Child* and founder of Texas Christian University's Institute of Child Development, used to say, "It's so awesome when science finally catches up to God." While *The New York Times* and researchers may be puzzled that both a mom and a dad matter to a balanced rearing of children, our God is not puzzled because this was His original design. A godly man will lead toward a strong family.

As I travel often for the work of Lifeline, my strong, capable, and supportive wife bears the brunt of my absence. My son struggles to lead his sisters lovingly resorting instead to ruling over them. My girls feel the threat to their safety and find themselves much more on edge. At the end of all of my trips my wife embraces me and says, "I thank our God I don't have to continue doing this without you." Beloved, our children need moms and our children need dads because this was the Creator's design.

Moms fulfill the inherent needs of their sons through their steadfast support. God created women to be natural nurturers, and in turn He created an insatiable need in boys for significance. When a mom looks at her young son and tells him how proud she is, the euphoria that is set off in his brain creates intense security. This need for significance follows boy all the way through manhood. The truth is that most men aren't drawn into adultery as much by physical desire, but by the woman who fulfills the need of significance.

That's why Solomon warns the wayward man in Proverbs 6:23-25 by saying,

> For the commandment is a lamp and the teaching a light,
> and the reproofs of discipline are the way of life,
> to preserve you from the evil woman,
> from the smooth tongue of the adulteress.
> Do not desire her beauty in your heart,
> and do not let her capture you with her eyelashes.

Then Solomon warns again in Proverbs 7:13-15,

> She seizes him and kisses him,
> and with bold face she says to him,
> I had to offer sacrifices,
> and today I have paid my vows;
> so now I have come out to meet you,
> to seek you eagerly, and I have found you.

Notice the first warnings that Solomon mentions before anything physical or sexual occurs—the woman has met the man's need of significance. The smooth tongue has praised him and told him he measures up. The woman has eagerly sought after him, which makes the man feel important.

Moms play such an important role of nurturing their sons, probing their hearts, and pointing them to significance that can ultimately only be found in a perfect parent. A good, good Father who says of all His children,

> Fear not, for I have redeemed you; I have called you by name, you are Mine. When you pass through the waters, I will be with you; and through the rivers, they shall not overwhelm you; when you walk through fire you shall not be burned, and the flame shall not consume you. For I am the Lord your God, the Holy One of Israel, your Savior.
> —Isaiah 43:1-3

Men, our significance ultimately must be found in Christ, because our families need us, our neighborhoods crave our influence, and the world needs our godly leadership. Dads provide so many rich things to their children, things that the Lord uniquely designed children to receive from Christ-fearing dads.

Daughters need security from their fathers. This security is not only physical but also emotional. While young boys crave significance, young women need emotional, physical, and spiritual protection. A young woman will never know her intrinsic beauty by trying to seek approval from the world. The first whispers that calm her anxious heart are from a daddy who constantly tells her she is beautiful and special. These whispers train her ears ultimately to hear the deafening roar of a Heavenly Father who calls her His beloved.

I am by no means a perfect father. I make many mistakes, lose my patience, and sometimes check out with the stress of the world, but one thing I make sure to do daily is rehearse with my two girls how much I love them, how precious they are intrinsically, and how astonishingly beautifully the Lord has created them. I love asking them, "How did you get to be so beautiful" and hearing them respond in kind, "because this is the way that God made me."

But the world is outright lying to our daughters. The world gives them a list of characteristics that are mandatory and impossible to keep. The reason why so many women struggle with eating disorders, huge esteem issues, and massive identity issues is because they have believed the lie that they don't and can't measure up. Know that the very first glance that our daughters and our children have of a Heavenly Father comes from His shadow which is viewed from earthly dads. We play such a large looming role in the lives of our children.

While sons desperately need significance from their moms, they need patient and firm instruction from their dads. In order to provide this, dads must be present in mind and body. All men need an example to follow, because while at the core we were born for adventure and conquest, we need to be pointed in the right direction. This is why when Jesus was choosing His 12 disciples He didn't just tell them what to do, but He told them, *"Follow me and I will make you fishers of men."*

Men, our sons will indelibly follow our lead. This is why they don't need men who are hypocrites, but men who are authentic, transparent, and honest with struggles while constantly pointing them to the right way.

I will never forget when my son was young, watching him imitate my every move. He wanted to dress like me, he liked the things I liked, and he followed me wherever I went. This, friends, is great accountability. I needed to be following Christ consistently, reading the Word daily, and praying without ceasing so that I could model the man that I pray he will become. Paul understands this when he says in 1 Corinthians 11:1: *"Be imitators of me, as I am of Christ."* So brothers, put down the smartphone, turn off the TV, and pick up a Bible. Life is short. Pray more. Read your Bible. Love your wife. Pay attention to your children.

As men and dads we are called to be leaders and particularly the leaders of our homes. God gives crucial instructions to His people in Deuteronomy 6 and specifically gives responsibility to godly men.

Hear, O Israel: The Lord our God, the Lord is one. You shall love the Lord your God with all your heart and with all your soul and with all your might. And these words that I command you today shall be on your heart. You shall teach them diligently to your children, and shall talk of them when you sit in your house, and when you walk by the way, and when you lie down, and when you rise. You shall bind them as a sign on your hand, and they shall be as frontlets between your eyes. You shall write them on the doorposts of your house and on your gates. —**Deuteronomy 6:4-9**

We need fathers who take the explicit instructions of this verse seriously and who implicitly love, lead, and show attention to their children. There are many helpful applications I have found on how to best do this for the three children the Lord has blessed Ashley and me to shepherd.

First, we must **make uninterrupted family meals a priority**. I am afraid that our homes revolve too much around entertainment and screens and less around undistracted conversation. We have learned so much about our children around the dinner table with the TV off, the music muted, and the devices far away. The Lord has designed our bodies to need fuel — we cannot survive without eating. This common daily occurrence provides excellent opportunities to relate spiritually, emotionally and physically with our children.

Second, we must **spend uninterrupted time with our children individually**. It has been through these times that both Ashley and I have learned so much about who the Lord has truly made our children to be. We have parent-child dates as often as we can. While there are certain parameters, the child gets to choose the activity and the meal. One year, in lieu of birthday gifts, we decided to take each child individually on an overnight trip to a nearby city. I cannot even begin to describe the value that those hours together provided us as parents. It was a true joy to spend undivided one on one time with each of our children. I would highly recommend investing in your children this way if at all possible. Even if you can't afford to make it an overnight stay in a hotel, take your child camping or take them out for a whole day together.

While test driving Ford F-150s when he was 10-years-old, Caleb and I first started to have those hard conversations about pornography. While being behind that muscle truck that every masculine man dreams of, I was able to explain the distortion of sexual intimacy that our adversary uses to rob the heart and joy of manly men. Then over wings we were able to talk about the beauty of women by looking at those characteristics that made his mom and sisters so special. Several years later we walked through a book called *13 Ways to Ruin Your Life* by my friend Jarrod Jones Pastor of Grace Community Church in Warwick, NY; and Caleb still remembered the night of Ford trucks and wings.

For my middle daughter, Adelynn, it was a night we visited a trampoline park. We talked until late at Starbucks about her fears, insecurities, and frustrations. That simple night of fun opened up the treasure trove of her heart and gave me the opportunity to affirm her, encourage her, and point her to Christ in a most authentic way.

And it has been the continuous dates to Emily's favorite Birmingham bakery, Edgars, that have given me the opportunity to hear her precious take on the world. As I enjoy this spunky and joyful little girl, the Lord has allowed me to affirm her and encourage her internal confidence that the Lord has created her uniquely and perfectly.

Third, we must **spend time reading to our children**. We must read fun and pointless books that make us belly laugh. We must read biographies about explorers, missionaries, and real people. However, it is imperative that we read the Word of God to our children. When our children were too young to even speak we read simple Bible stories to them from children's Bibles with colorful pictures. As they grew we received the gift of Sally Lloyd Jones' *The Jesus Storybook Bible: Every Story Whispers His Name*. Even through all of these paraphrases and wonderfully written children's books, our children still need to hear us read aloud the actual Word of God. If you don't know where to start, begin in one of the Johns — The Gospel of John or 1 John.

Fourth, we must **pray for and with our children**. If we are not modeling dependence on God to our children then they will never understand how to rely upon the Father. During the summer of 2016, finances were extremely tight at Lifeline and the stress was overwhelming. Over dinner, in age appropriate ways, we included the children in on what was happening and asked them to pray with us and for us. Emily would ask the Lord "to provide Lifeline with more zeros." In her youthful innocence she understood that we needed more than just $1 or $10, but $100s and $1,000s.

That summer was one of the hardest financial challenges we have been faced with as a ministry. Summer is always a leaner time but that summer was coupled with the uncertainty which comes from a presidential election. One week we had a very specific need and were short about $10,000. Ashley and I had been fasting and praying over the need and including the children.

When the day came on which the money was being demanded, the money didn't come. As I was driving home that afternoon, I cried out to God just as I entered my neighborhood. I told the Lord, "I am desperate and I don't know what to do. I still trust You and know that You can provide this need, but I don't understand and I'm upset. I am going to praise You no matter Your answer, but Father, I just need to know that You hear me."

Within seconds my phone vibrated with a text message from a friend which read, "I just wanted you to know that the Lord pricked our hearts yesterday to give $10,000 and so we went online this morning to give it, we are praying for you." Tears began to well in my eyes as I turned the corner to my house. Then my kids were standing in the front yard holding signs which read, "We love you Daddy. We are praying for you. God hears you. God is in control." They had been waiting for 45 minutes for me to come home.

That night we all celebrated that our Father hears us when we pray and that He provides. If we had not included our children in the struggle, we would have robbed them of an opportunity to depend on the Lord. They also may not have understood why Daddy was stressed or seen their parents trust not in themselves, but in a sovereign, holy and faithful God.

Fifth, we need to **play with our children**. We need to enter into their world, their likes, and their interests. I love playing basketball with my son and playing card games with my daughters. Many times I am the customer at their restaurant or the toddler who calls them "mom". We laugh together and we enjoy one another. I am not embarrassed by my children, but I am overjoyed to be in relationship with them.

One night, Emily decided that Adelynn, Caleb, and I needed to be her dogs. It was all fun and games until she announced she was taking us on a walk around our new neighborhood with our makeshift leashes. We all went along with her plan and laughed until we cried as cars drove by and gave us puzzled and bewildered looks.   That night we had such an awesome conversation about how some people wouldn't understand our faith, love, and devotion to Jesus. As we rely on Jesus some people would be puzzled, some would laugh, and some would be bewildered; however, we must not be ashamed of the gospel because it is the power of God unto salvation (Romans 1:18).

And finally, we must **continually speak of Jesus to our children**. We must use every opportunity and experience to sow gospel threads into their hearts. Every sunset is an opportunity to praise the grandeur of God. Every adventure provides a great time to talk about a God who pursues us with reckless abandon. We must speak of Jesus constantly to our children. As dads, we serve our wives wholeheartedly when we partner with her in these ways to raise our children.

As godly men we must humbly serve and protect the weak, the vulnerable and the orphan. We must seek integrity in every area of our lives. And we must lead our families, communities, churches, and businesses with courage and conviction. We are God's image bearers of justice and strength to a watching world. We are called to bring strength and stability to our families.

The Lord is a stronghold for the oppressed, a stronghold in times of trouble. —**Psalm 9:9**

And brothers, when we come alongside children who are fatherless, we can love them in the same ways we love the children who live in our homes. We must take the lead and initiative to serve orphans and vulnerable children and not wait for our wives to coax us to get engaged.

I love the practical nature of the Book of Ruth. We meet Ruth in Chapter 1. She is a Moabite who marries an Israelite. This would not be dissimilar to a 20th Century Jew marrying a Nazi. There was intense hatred among the Jews and Moabites. In very short order practically and functionally, Ruth becomes a widow, a stranger, an alien, and an orphan in 22 verses.

With unabashed resolution she follows her mother-in-law away from her homeland of Moab into Israel. She says in Ruth 1:16: *"Do not urge me to leave you or to return from following you. For where you go I will go, and where you lodge I will lodge. Your people shall be my people, and your God my God."*

It's funny how many times this verse is quoted in marriage ceremonies, because this statement was made from a woman to her mother-in-law. So rarely today would you ever hear anyone pledge this kind of unwavering affection to his or her mother-in-law.

Then in Ruth Chapter 2, Ruth follows her mother-in-law into the land of Israel. And in God's great sovereignty, Ruth ends up in the field of a man named Boaz. In the fields of Boaz, we see the commands of Deuteronomy 24:17-21 lived out in practicality toward Ruth — a stranger, alien, orphan and widow.

> *When you reap your harvest in your field and forget a sheaf in the field, you shall not go back to get it. It shall be for the sojourner, the fatherless, and the widow, that the Lord your God may bless you in all the work of your hands.* —**Deuteronomy 24:19**

There are five practical things that Boaz, a man of God, does for Ruth that the Church and godly men must imitate on behalf of the fatherless.

First, we must **take notice of the fatherless**. In Ruth 2:5-8, Boaz takes notice of Ruth. She is not invisible to him, and she is not an inconvenience either.

So many times the fatherless and the vulnerable feel invisible. We show them dignity by taking notice.

Second, we must **begin to provide for the fatherless** by inviting them to eat with us, by helping with their basic needs, and by spiritually leading them. In Ruth 2:17-19, Boaz invites Ruth to sit at his table and to share a meal with him and his family. This would have been scandalous and counter-cultural in those times, but the love of God trumps culture. Church, are we willing to inconvenience ourselves and our comfort in order to show the love of God to those in the greatest need? We must provide for the fatherless.

Third, we must **bless, affirm, and encourage the fatherless and their families.** So many times the needy, the broken, and the downtrodden have no one to speak truth to them and to remind them that they are created in the image of Almighty God. Speaking an affirmation and a blessing over a vulnerable child is akin to pouring water onto a parched land — the land and the child will soak it up immediately. Boaz takes the time to notice the sacrifice that Ruth had made on behalf of Naomi. He took the time to make sure he told her the value and worth which she possessed.

Again, are we willing to invest our time and lives to not just throw money at problems but to get our hands dirty and our lives engaged? Words of affirmation are so powerful to children and their families. Many times they have begun to believe the lie that their life is invaluable and that they will never amount to anything. We combat this affront when we speak, bless, affirm, and encourage their hearts with truth.

Fourth, our churches and our families must **protect the fatherless.** Certainly this includes physically protecting by helping mothers secure better jobs, helping single parent families find safer neighborhoods, and in general defending these children. Physical protection is extremely important to mental well-being. While I may not be the most imposing of physical specimens, my children rest easier when I am home. When they were younger they thought I could conquer anything; now that they are older they just have the confidence that I would do anything humanly possible to protect them. Daddies provide protection and when dad is missing, safety can be an issue. Women are preyed upon by predators who will also prey on their children.

Protection isn't just physical. It is also social in protecting the honor and dignity of the fatherless. Protection is also emotional, mental, and spiritual. Jesus knew when He sent out His disciples that He was sending them out to the "wolves." He knew that in the world there were those who would break the spirit even while not touching the body. We must protect the spirit and emotions of the vulnerable by being as "innocent as doves but as wise as serpents."

Paul gives us a good example of this in Acts 20 when he departs from the Ephesians after spending three years among them. He says in verse 31-32:

> Therefore be alert, remembering that for three years I did not cease night or day to admonish every one with tears. And now I commend you to God and to the word of His grace, which is able to build you up and to give you the inheritance among all those who are sanctified.

Paul also knew that, *"after my departure fierce wolves will come in among you, not sparing the flock; and from among your own selves will arise men speaking twisted things, to draw away the disciples after them."* (Acts 20:29-30)

We protect the hearts, minds and souls of the fatherless by investing in them, by teaching them God's truth found in the Bible, by praying over them and for them, and by continually pointing them to God the Father. We also make sure that we help network them with others who will also take care of them. In Ruth 2:9, Boaz instructs his young men to protect and defend Ruth. We must use our networks and relationships to defend the fatherless.

Fifth, we must show honor to the fatherless and their families by **bringing them into our sphere of influence and inviting them into our homes.** Shortly after Hurricane Katrina ravaged New Orleans, Ashley and I were visiting my parents one Sunday morning. While we were there we met a disheveled man named George Bey. He was easily identifiable as a refugee of the storm. After the Sunday morning services we rushed over, introduced ourselves, heard his story, and then invited him to come to lunch with us. Instantly his countenance changed. We learned that George had never been married and had no immediate family since his parents had passed when he was a teenager.

After lunch, my parents continued to introduce George to folks within their local church. George was invited into homes, given a job, and established as a part of the church community. Shortly after visiting Tuscaloosa, Alabama, George set up roots, surrendered his life to Christ, joined the church, began singing in the choir, and joined a faith family. Unfortunately, a few years later George passed away. I was unable to attend his funeral, but that was okay, because this man with no family had a packed out service attended by his faith family.

Boaz brings Ruth into his community, he gives her the place of honor at his table, and then he gives her a to go box of food. He honors this woman from the rival land of Moab and he shows her grace, mercy, and love. We must be willing to invite the fatherless in.

Brothers, in all of these things we find in Ruth 2 notice that Boaz is the initiator. This godly man takes the lead and ultimately a strong family is created, because godly men equal strong families. We need to begin wrapping around fatherless families today, because this is what those made in the image of God do. We fight for life outside of the womb as passionately as we do for the life when it is inside the womb, because both are equally vulnerable.

Discussion Questions

1. How does Genesis 3 inform us that the pro-life movement is not just a "woman's issue" but also an "apathy of man issue"?

2. It was God's design for our children to need moms and dads. For families who are without one of those roles due to death or circumstance, how can we stand in the gap to love and help lead them?

3. In what ways is the world lying to our children? How can we combat that with the Truth of God's Word and our example to follow it?

4. What are some practical ways you can live out Deuteronomy 6:4-9?

5. Reflecting on the five things Boaz did for Ruth, which ones seem practical for you to do for the fatherless now? Do any of them seem daunting at first glance?

Chapter Eight

LIFE IS PRECIOUS

All life is not equal. That's a difficult thing for liberals like me
to talk about, lest we wind up looking like death-panel-loving,
kill-your-grandma and your-precious-baby storm troopers. Yet a
fetus can be a human life without having the same rights as the
woman in whose body it resides. She's the boss. Her life and
what is right for her circumstances and
her health should automatically trump the rights of the
non-autonomous entity inside of her. Always.

— Mary Elizabeth Williams, "So What If Abortion Ends Life?"

Late in the summer of 2017, an article was published by CBS News about the almost complete eradication of Down syndrome babies through genetic testing and elective abortion in Iceland. According to the article, over 99% of the babies with Down syndrome were aborted.

The article reports,

> With the rise of prenatal screening tests across Europe and the U.S., the number of babies born with Down syndrome has significantly decreased, but few countries have come as close to eradicating Down syndrome births as Iceland. According to the most recent data available, the U.S. has an estimated termination rate for Down syndrome of 67%. In France, it's 77%. In Denmark, it's 98%. The law in Iceland permits abortion after 16 weeks if the fetus has a deformity, and Down syndrome is included in this category.

Geneticist Kari Stefansson, quoted in the article, is said to have a unique perspective on the advancement of medical technology.

> My understanding is that we have basically eradicated, almost, Down syndrome from our society, that there is hardly ever a child with Down syndrome in Iceland anymore. I don't think there's anything wrong with aspiring to have healthy children.

> A woman who made the decision to abort her baby who had a gene deficiency said, "This is your life! You have the right to choose how your life will look. We don't look at abortion as murder, we look at it like a thing we ended. We ended a possible life that may have had huge complications, preventing suffering for the child and for the family. I think that's more of a right than seeing it as a murder. It's not so black and white — life isn't black and white. Life is gray."

Let's have grace for this woman, but let's also hear how polluted our world, society and culture has become. Life is no longer viewed as precious or sacred. Beloved, we are on a truly slippery slope when young women and culture is praised for saying that life is "gray."

On the contrary, life is utterly precious because it reflects the glory and image of our great God. When we see the Down syndrome abortion rate skyrocket to almost 100% in Iceland, we need to know that we are not created by our own effort or by accident. We are not created in the womb simply by a conjugal act of a mom and a dad. We are created in the womb by a loving Father who knits us together, who forms us like a Potter, and who fashions us in His image — no matter the syndrome we may have.

When we see children or adults with Down syndrome, we must look upon them as precious because they are no less an image bearer than those of us without Down syndrome. All life is precious and we must speak up to defend it.

I've traveled around the world, and in every country I've seen little babies, children and teenagers with Down syndrome. They are some of the most precious children. It breaks my heart to think of all the families, redeemed by the gospel of Jesus Christ, who are ready to adopt those children and bring them into their home who may not have the opportunity.

One of my dear friends, a pastor in Kansas, has brought home two precious daughters from Asia with Down syndrome. While brought home at different times, these girls are identical in age and are the most precious twinned sisters you can imagine. These girls love life to the fullest. Certainly their struggle at times is real, but they are not defined by a syndrome. They are marked by a family, by a Savior, and by joy. I love hearing the stories from my friend about the simplicity and authenticity that his girls speak about Christ, the gospel and God's Word.

Life is Precious

Since the beginning of time there has been a war led by Satan against children. Most notably, Pharaoh orders the destruction of all the boy Israelite babies in Exodus 1:15-16, and then Herod orders the slaughter of all the boys two years and younger in Bethlehem in Matthew 2:16. Both of these leaders order these executions for fear that their power would be threatened — they were so power hungry that life was just an obstacle to obliterate. Satan will use whatever means necessary to twist the minds of people in order to destroy God's image bearers.

In his book *Adopted for Life*, Dr. Russell Moore says,

> *Whether through political machinations such as those of Pharaoh and Herod, through military conquests in which bloodthirsty armies rip babies from pregnant mothers' wombs (Amos 1:13), or through the more "routine" seeming family disintegration and family chaos, children are always hurt. Human history is riddled with their corpses ... The demonic powers hate babies because they hate Jesus. When they destroy "the least of these" (Matthew 25:40, 45), the most vulnerable among us, they're destroying a picture of Jesus Himself.*

The common link between Pharaoh and Herod's orders is that God made a way forward and a way of escape for deliverance. The Lord thwarted the plan of Satan both times through a physical family and physical adoption.

> Then the king of Egypt said to the Hebrew midwives, one of whom was named Shiphrah and the other Puah, "When you serve as midwife to the Hebrew women and see them on the birthstool, if it is a son, you shall kill him, but if it is a daughter, she shall live." —**Exodus 1:15-16**

Exodus goes on to record that the midwives feared God and did not comply with the order of Pharaoh but instead allowed the babies to live. These fearless women did not bow a knee to the world order of the day when it was in direct violation with the precepts of God. These women stood in the gap and many children were spared because of their integrity.

We have women like these today. Women who are standing in the gap for life. They include women who work, counsel, or volunteer at crisis pregnancy centers as well as women who counsel young moms toward adoption when it's the best option.

Yahweh provides even more relief to the slaughter of innocent Hebrew babies as He provides godly moms who are willing to protect innocent life at all costs. Exodus begins Chapter 2 by telling us that a Levite woman gave birth to a beautiful baby boy whom she hid for three months. However, when she could no longer hide the baby Moses, she gently knit together a basket, put the baby in the basket, and then delicately placed the basket along the banks of the Nile. For an extra measure of protection, this woman who is never mentioned by name, set her older daughter Miriam to watch over her baby brother.

Oh beloved, there are women today who find themselves in terrible predicaments. These women find themselves pregnant, looking for love in the wrong places, and many times abused or manipulated. However, when these women choose life for their child, we need to recognize them as heroes. In a culture of death, these women, many of whom we may never know by name, bring life to their children when abortion has become so convenient and acceptable. Abortion is the "easy" way out, but the women who choose life are brave and courageous. These are some of the fiercest champions of life who are on the front lines. We must pray for them and honor them. These women are true heroes.

Beyond providing alternatives to abortion, our great God provides in another way to defend His image bearers. The Lord brings forth adoption. As the narrative unfolds in Exodus 2, we see baby Moses drawn out of the water by none other than Pharaoh's daughter. She sees this Hebrew baby and instantly knows that a loving birth mother took painstaking care to preserve his life. Ironically, baby Moses becomes a member of the household of the king of Egypt — the adopted son.

And of course the Lord would use this adoption story to preserve the lives of so many more. The Lord would use Moses to free His people the Israelites from Egypt. Moses would stand before Pharaoh multiple times and command that he let the people go. How was a Hebrew slave able to approach such a power hungry king, have an audience, and not be punished? Well, Moses wasn't just approaching any king, he was approaching his uncle, through the beautiful and messy story of adoption.

Because Moses had this audience, the Lord used ten plagues and many signs and wonders to free His chosen people — the 12 tribes of Israel. One of those tribes was the tribe of Judah. Don't miss this: this very tribe would birth the kings of Israel, but most importantly, this tribe would bring forth King Jesus. Through adoption, the Lord preserved His people and the salvation of the world.

Adoption also plays heavily into the scene we find with Herod in Matthew 2:16 when Matthew's gospel tells us,

> *Then Herod, when he saw that he had been tricked by the wise men, became furious, and he sent and killed all the male children in Bethlehem and in all that region who were two years old or under, according to the time that he had ascertained from the wise men.*

Herod learned from the wise men that a star had shone bright over David's town, Bethlehem, to lead the way to the future King of the Jews. This left Herod incredulous — he was the rightful king of the Jews. In an attempt to protect his lineage and power, he orders the execution of all boy babies.

Oh, but the unfolding plan of God could never be stopped nor thwarted by Satan. God the Father would protect His son, the ultimate defender of the *Imago Dei*. The Savior King was the one who had come to give true life to all image bearers, but until Jesus began that work, His earthly protector was a simple carpenter from Nazareth named Joseph.

Before Herod's sinister plan, God had called out to Joseph in a dream and asked him to take Mary, his betrothed as his wife, and the child through her unexpected pregnancy, as his own. Joseph was a noble man. He was betrothed to Mary before this unplanned pregnancy and was going to quietly divorce her instead of having her executed as the law required.

Joseph obeys God, protects Mary, and provides for her during her pregnancy. Then, on a frantic and crazy night, the King of the World appears through a simple girl tucked away in a cave surrounded by animals. Joseph was an adoptive dad in one unexpected, zany, and holy adoption journey.

However, this adoption was utterly important to the mission and divine plan of God. First, it was through Joseph that Jesus met the lineage requirement for the Messiah. In Matthew 1 we learn that Abraham had Isaac; Isaac was Judah's grandfather; Judah's line led to King David; and then a humble carpenter named Joseph, the grandson of Matthan, came from the direct line of King David. Joseph was the earthly father of the King of all Kings and the Lord of all Lords, King Jesus the Messiah.

Looking on in Matthew 2, before Herod issues his deathly decree against boys under two, God warns Joseph in a dream saying, *"Rise, take the child and his mother, and flee to Egypt, and remain there until I tell you, for Herod is about to search for the child, to destroy him."*

Immediately, Joseph, accustomed to God speaking truth through dreams, flees to Egypt and protects the child, exactly what any parent would do if their child was in danger. Because of this safe passage to Egypt, the King of the World, who had humbled Himself to the likeness of man, was protected at His most vulnerable state, and all of this through earthly, physical adoption.

Beloved, know that one of God's great gifts is physical adoption of children. Through adoption we protect God's image bearers and prove that abortion is irrelevant. Adoption is blessed by God and used by Him for the proclamation of His glorious gospel.

He is God and We Are Not

We are not sovereign, and we are not in control. We have no idea what the future holds. For example, my wife Ashley and I have dear friends with three young children. Towards the end of 2018, the wife was told her cancer wasn't treatable and that her only hope was to manage potential pain. This young mother and wife went through the painstaking process of making videos for her kids, taking the "last" family photos, and preparing for an extraordinary exit from this life.

Her treatment plan called for one last visit to MD Anderson in Houston, Texas. It was one last shot to see if modern medicine truly had failed our friends. Back in Birmingham we were hoping for a miracle but praying for wisdom, strength and grace for a husband, a wife, a dad, a mom, and three precious children.

I dropped my phone when the text came across with report from MD Anderson, "We just got scan results. We have been given a gift! There is no cancer. We are in shock. The doctor was in shock. It is a good day!! Hallelujah!!!"

The doctors in Houston were so stunned that before giving the results they went back to compare these scans with the earlier scans. They verified the surgery scars and the identifying factors, and sure enough, there was no cancer.

Beloved, we do not know what our God can and will do. We think modern medicine is a savior and so advanced, when in reality it is just an instrument in the hand of our sovereign God. Life is far too precious for us to play god. Life *is* black and white, and an abortion of a child simply because they have a syndrome, disability, or gene deficiency *is* murder. It's not "a thing ended."

In August 2017, the world discovered the story of Charlie Gard in the United Kingdom. Charlie's parents were fighting courts to first, allow them to take him to the U.S. for specialized treatment that might save his life. Second, a mom and dad were fighting the courts for the right to take Charlie home to spend his last days in peace. Both requests were denied by British courts, signifying that Charlie's life wasn't worth the hassle.

Charlie's parents said in a statement after his death, "We just want some peace with our son, no hospital, no lawyers, no courts, no media, just quality time with Charlie away from everything to say goodbye to him in the most loving way." They continued, "Mummy and Daddy love you so much Charlie, we always have and we always will and we are so sorry that we couldn't save you. We had the chance but we weren't allowed to give you that chance. Sweet dreams baby. Sleep tight our beautiful little boy, you are our hero."

Charlie was diagnosed with Mitochondrial DNA depletion syndrome, a condition that causes muscle weakness and loss of motor skills. In the end, British courts said his life wasn't worthy of the fight.

Our great God disagrees vehemently with the courts when He says in Jeremiah 1:5, *"Before I formed you in the womb I knew you, and before you were born I consecrated you; I appointed you a prophet to the nations."* And then again in Jeremiah 44:2-3, *"Thus says the Lord who made you, who formed you from the womb and will help you: Fear not, O Jacob my servant, Jeshurun whom I have chosen. For I will pour water on the thirsty land, and streams on the dry ground; I will pour my Spirit upon your offspring, and my blessing on your descendants."*

Beloved, we must speak up for the dignity of all life. We must speak up against abortion, genocide, and euthanasia, so our defending of life doesn't stop at birth. We must continue to support those children and their birth families once they are born. We need to support spiritually, physically, and emotionally impoverished families by equipping them to care for their children.

We need to walk alongside women who choose life by discipling them, mentoring them, and ultimately being present for them. We need to provide a home to children through foster care. When it is appropriate, we must adopt children either domestically, or from foster care, or internationally. We must never judge the value of life by a physical, mental, or emotional disability, but by the sanctity of life placed upon that life by God.

We are not just pro-birth; we are life-affirming. Therefore, we fiercely defend life. *The New York Post* released an article in November 2018 titled, "Doctors Probed for Euthanizing Autistic Woman." The article shook me to the core and brought me to my knees in tears as it reports, "In Belgium and the Netherlands, it is legal for doctors to euthanize patients who have psychiatric problems that cause 'unbearable and untreatable' suffering. Among Belgians put to death for mental health reasons, the most common conditions are depression, personality disorder and Asperger's, a mild form of autism."

The article goes on to report that once euthanization was legalized in Belgium in 2002, more than 10,000 people have been killed at the hands of doctors. Under the law, psychiatrists are allowed to suggest euthanization to their patients or next of kin if the patient doesn't possess the cognizance to make the decision. The doctor at the center of the article was being accused of too quickly approving euthanasia requests from patients with Asperger's.

This article is an example of how our sin and apathy on the issues of life have led to a completely low view of lives which are not deemed healthy or perfect. No man has the right, the authority, or the ability to ever deem any life worthy or unworthy of living because that authority rests solely with the King of Kings and the Lord of Lords.

My dear brother, Dr. Rick Morton, author of *Orphanology* and *KnowOrphans* has adopted three precious children from Ukraine with his sweet wife Denise. Their first child to come into their home is one of the most brilliant electricians and plumbers that I have ever met. Erick is a teenager who loves Alabama football, his two dogs, his family, and all things that relate to plumbing and electricity. Erick has been to my home many times to fix our garbage disposal, fluorescent lights, dishwasher, and many other things. Here is the thing. Erick owes many of his exceptional abilities and interests to Asperger's Syndrome.

Although Erick is still a teenager, I am abundantly confident that the Lord will use this young man for unimaginable purposes. *The New York Post* article damages my heart and emotions because in Belgium or the Netherlands it is possible that a psychiatrist might suggest the unthinkable for someone with Asperger's. This isn't just a nebulous diagnosis to me. This unique set of gifts and abilities and maybe a few limitations has a name and a face for me in the precious life of Erick. They aren't really providing euthanasia or eradicating genetic anomalies in these nations that practice selective abortions. They are really just using a fancy word that means "murder."

Beloved, we cannot just sit by and be silent. In Belgium alone, 625 people have been killed each year from this asinine law. The population of Belgium is similar in size to that of Houston, Texas. If we knew on average two people were being murdered daily in Houston, we would surely take action. It is no different if you know in your city that on average two babies were aborted daily. You would speak out. We speak out because life is utterly precious.

At the church I attend in Birmingham, The Church at Brook Hills, we recently had the great opportunity to watch a 40-year-old man with Turner syndrome walk through the baptism waters. While this syndrome has been debilitating to him both physically and cognitively, he gives his testimony that Jesus Christ is his Lord and Savior. I know other men and women with Down syndrome who are confessing today that Jesus Christ is their Lord and Savior.

Beloved, we must speak up. We must wrap our lives around those who have genetic differences and named syndromes. We must wrap our lives around those who this world and culture are calling "special needs." We must love them with our lives, and we must love them with the gospel. If you want to get engaged with your life and your family, to show that you believe that children, families, teenagers and adults with Down syndrome, Turner syndrome or any other syndrome are worth the fight, then take the first step today to adopt or foster a child, walk alongside families who have children with needs, or volunteer in your church's special needs ministry. By taking personal action, we ultimately show the world that all life counts.

Discussion Questions

1. Knowing the pro-life movement is as old as the Old Testament, how are you encouraged and motived by scripture to continue the fight?

2. God's unfolding plan of redemption could not be stopped by Pharaoh, Herod, or Satan himself. How does God's redemption strategy speak to His love for adoption?

3. How does being pro-life extend to caring for someone after birth? How can we also continue to be life-affirming for families who choose life?

4. Believing that all life is precious, how can we invest in those with genetic differences or syndromes? How can we love them and their families well and affirm the truth that they are also Image bearers of our holy God?

Chapter Nine

ADOPTION AND ORPHAN CARE

*Wash yourselves; make yourselves clean; remove the evil of your
deeds from before My eyes; cease to do evil, learn to do good;
seek justice, correct oppression;
bring justice to (defend) the fatherless, plead the widow's cause.*

— Isaiah 1:16-17

During the summer of 2014, my family was hosting my previously mentioned brother from Uganda, Pastor Raphael Kajjubi, along with his delightful wife Allen. In general, I have experienced African believers to be extremely conservative, which is beneficial because our family is about as conservative as you can get. That is except for my precocious daughter, Emily. She was four at the time, and one night after dinner, Ashley asked the kids to go put their pajamas on.

The next thing we know, Emily bounded down the stairs much too quickly, draped in nothing but the rug from her room and a single pair of white socks. I feel the blood rushing from my face, as she proceeds to drop the rug to the floor and exclaim, "Look, I'm naked!" as if that was not abundantly clear.

Ashley and I both held our breath in sheer horror, believing that we had single handedly destroyed the relationship with Lifeline's dearest orphan care partner and this brother of mine. It was an epic international incident in the Newell kitchen.

Slowly, we opened our eyes to look on in horror at our gentle guests from Africa. Instead of shock, we were relieved to begin to hear them rolling in laughter. Ashley quickly ushered Emily back up the stairs, and Raphael admitted, "My brother, she is just like our three year old daughter Delight. We were so worried she would do the exact same thing to you when you stayed with us in our home last month." Then Allen chimed in, "Those girls are so much alike, they just might be twins."

Beloved, one thing I have learned over my 16 years of ministry with Lifeline is that children are similar no matter the context, culture, or background. Children are unpredictable and curious. They have wild imaginations, and they desperately want to be loved. Every child gets scared, has dreams and fears, and every last one has a hole in their hearts that only the gospel of Christ can fill.

One thing, however, that separates orphans, foster children, and vulnerable children from my own children is that they lack the support of family. Our goal and aim as the Bride of Christ must be to disciple these children and their families while displaying the love of Christ.

Child Welfare and Gospel-Drive Justice

We must understand that the chief need of a child is not food, shelter, or stability. Their chief need is the gospel. These children's physical needs are vital, but they can only truly be addressed correctly through the lens of gospel transformation.

It is not the responsibility of governments to care for children; it's not the responsibility of the elite; it's not even the responsibility of humanitarians; but it is the command given directly to God's redeemed people.

Cleary, God tells His people through the prophet Isaiah in Isaiah 1:16-17 to take their eyes off themselves and to cease doing evil; however, then the Lord gives them a charge to replace their evil and selfish deeds. They are to seek justice, do good for the vulnerable, and defend the fatherless.

Likewise, the prophet Micah says in Micah 6:8: *"He has told you, O man, what is good; and what does the Lord require of you but to do justice, and to love kindness, and to walk humbly with your God?"*

The command to care for orphans, the vulnerable, the stranger and the widow is echoed throughout the Old Testament, as God continually reminds his people, "I redeemed you from slavery for My glory and for My name. You show people to whom you belong by your action."

The only commands of God that we actually demonstrate that we believe are those that we obey. The way we show our allegiance to the Lord is through our participation in His work. We weren't given the Bible just to read and study. We were given the Bible to put it into action. Our study and reading is so that we act on the imperatives and conform to the image of Christ.

Beloved, the Word of God is full of imperatives toward gospel-driven justice for the orphan and vulnerable, and gospel-centered justice is utterly pro-life. When we show the gospel to vulnerable children and their families, we are showing them that we truly believe that all life bears the image of a Creator. Can you really call yourself pro-life if you decry abortion but turn a blind eye to those who have chosen life and are struggling?

I love how Matt Chandler, pastor of The Village Church in Dallas, Texas, explains why we step into gospel-driven justice. He says,

> *We live open-handed lives and seek to spot injustice and despair around us, and we enter into sorrow and pain so that the love, mercy, and beauty of God's reconciling work in Christ can be seen in our lives in the hopes that a broken world will see and give praise to God.*

The Old Testament is full of commands to care for the fatherless, which is how I will refer to these children throughout the rest of this chapter. Foster children, orphans, and vulnerable children usually all fit under the biblical heading of "fatherless." Even if they have a living father, they are functionally fatherless. Often that father is absent or even when he is present, he is so driven to despair that he can't adequately provide for his children tangibly, emotionally, or spiritually.

Our God is passionate for the fatherless and His passion is central to our understanding of His character. This is why we see Him say about Himself in Psalm 68:5-6a, *"Father of the fatherless and protector of widows is God in His holy habitation. God settles the solitary in a home."*

There is a thread that runs throughout the Old Testament of God calling His people to emulate His character by caring for the fatherless. We see the commands of Deuteronomy 24:17-22 echoed throughout the Pentateuch to God's chosen people:

> *You shall not pervert the justice due to the sojourner or to the fatherless, or take a widow's garment in pledge, but you shall remember that you were a slave in Egypt and the Lord your God redeemed you from there; therefore I command you to do this. "When you reap your harvest in your field and forget a sheaf in the field, you shall not go back to get it. It shall be for the sojourner, the fatherless, and the widow, that the Lord your God may bless you in all the work of your hands. When you beat your olive trees, you shall not go over them again. It shall be for the sojourner, the fatherless, and the widow. When you gather the grapes of your vineyard, you shall not strip it afterward. It shall be for the sojourner, the fatherless, and the widow. You shall remember that you were a slave in the land of Egypt; therefore I command you to do this."*

These commands extend into the New Testament and are most clearly stated in James 1:27 when James says, *"Religion that is pure and undefiled before God, the Father, is this: to visit orphans and widows in their affliction, and to keep oneself unstained from the world."*

This verse is a call to gospel-driven justice for the orphan and the widow, and also a call to personal holiness and gospel proclamation. The tendency is to only pay attention to the second half of James 1:27, yet we need not neglect the first part as well. It's a call to both personal holiness and pursuing justice. Our churches do a fine job preaching on personal holiness while most often ignoring our gospel-driven duty to care for the vulnerable. In fact, we would think a preacher to be a hypocrite if he said that personal holiness was only for a select group in the church and wasn't something for everyone; however, too often we view the call to care for the fatherless as a call only for a select group. The hypocrisy of personal holiness only being required of a few believers really helps us see the ridiculousness of limiting an imperative from Scripture to a select few in the Church.

God Visited So We Visit

So while acknowledging the universal call to personal holiness, let us look at the first half of James 1:27 with the same universal nature for all believers. Specifically, let's examine the phrase "to visit" or "to look after." This means "to take responsibility for their needs, to go to them and to take responsibility for them."

According to James, a religion that God our Father accepts as pure and faultless is this: to go to orphans and widows, and not just visit them, but to take ownership and responsibility for their needs; to go to them with deep concern. That's the kind of religion that our God and Father accepts.

The type of visiting James speaks of is found in a few other places throughout the Old and New Testaments. First, in Genesis 50:24-25: "*And Joseph said to his brothers, 'I am about to die, but God will **visit** you and bring you up out of this land to the land that He swore to Abraham, to Isaac, and to Jacob.' Then Joseph made the sons of Israel swear, saying, 'God will surely visit you, and you shall carry up my bones from here.'*"

At the end of his life, Joseph was assuring the people that God would come and take care of His people. Again, this wasn't a simple visit to someone's home; this was an abiding. Joseph was saying, "God's going to come to you. He's going to look after you. He's going to take responsibility for your needs. He is going to care for you with a deep concern."

Once more we see this concept of visitation in Psalm 8:3-4 where it says, *"When I look at Your heavens, the work of Your fingers, the moon and the stars, which You have set in place, what is man that You are mindful of him, and the son of man that You care for him?"*

James uses the Greek equivalent to these Hebrew words in James 1:27. God in His greatness and splendor, the Author, Creator, and Sustainer of the universe, steps down to look after us, **visit** us, and show deep concern for us.

In like manner, we see the Greek word used again in Luke 1:68, where Zechariah says, *"Blessed be the Lord God of Israel, for He has **visited** and redeemed His people."*

This is Zechariah giving praise to God for the birth of his son, John the Baptist. Literally the Lord came in the form of Jesus to **visit**, care for, and redeem His people. Zechariah saw that the Messiah had come in the way He fulfilled the birth of John to barren Elizabeth.

Similarly, we see this same Greek word in Matthew 25:36 and 25:43 in the famous parable of the sheep and the goats. Those who did unto the least of these inherited the kingdom of God. Those who did not do unto the least of these were separated from the presence of God.

> *"I was naked and you clothed Me, I was sick and you **visited** Me, I was in prison and you came to Me."* —**Matthew 25:36**

> *"I was a stranger and you did not welcome Me, naked and you did not clothe Me, sick and in prison and you did not **visit** Me."* —**Matthew 25:43**

This same word in Hebrew and Greek from the Old Testament and the New Testament is teaching us that God is consistent in His character, is concerned about looking after His people, and is coming to His people and caring for them. Through James, God is telling us that religion which is pure and true is that which goes to the neediest, the orphan and the widow, and cares for them.

However, beloved, we can deduce that the opposite of true religion is a religion that ignores, forgets, and neglects those who are needy, sick, and hungry as well as the poor, the orphans, and the widows. So I ask, do we as a Church have true religion or false religion? Are we truly protecting the *Imago Dei* imprinted on the most vulnerable, or are we turning a blind eye out of convenience?

Let us not miss the reason God commands His people to care for the fatherless. The chief aim of our care for the fatherless should be to proclaim the glory and gospel of Christ. We visit and care because He first visited and cared for us.

The Meek are Called to Care for the Fatherless

With this framework, I want us to see this precious truth found in one of the minor prophets, Zephaniah. Here we see how the gospel cries out for meek followers to humble themselves, realize their condition of sin, and trust no longer in themselves but in the hope of the nations, Jesus the Christ. Adoption and caring for the fatherless is ultimately a picture of the redemption we receive through the gospel.

Sin is crushing and defeating. We have been born into a life of sin, self-gratification, self-exaltation, and self-idolatry. To see the gospel is to realize the rightful King of the World stooped down to become like us. He came to the humble town of Bethlehem, on an ordinary and nondescript night, in order to make a world marked by sin and death, a world that would be redeemed.

Jesus came as a baby, but being God, He could have come as a full-grown man. He could have come at Passover or at the prescribed Feast. Instead,

He comes especially meekly. Through His ministry He calls out for the meek. He commands His followers to love and care for the outcast and the fatherless.

We have been called to a ministry of manifesting the gospel to the stranger, outcast, and alien in hopes of seeing the gospel go to all peoples, tribes, tongues, and nations.

Zephaniah 3:1-8 starts off:

> Woe to her who is rebellious and defiled, the oppressing city! She listens to no voice; she accepts no correction. She does not trust in the Lord; she does not draw near to her God.

> Her officials within her are roaring lions; her judges are evening wolves that leave nothing till the morning. Her prophets are fickle, treacherous men; her priests profane what is holy; they do violence to the law. The Lord within her is righteous; He does no injustice; every morning He shows forth His justice; each dawn He does not fail; but the unjust knows no shame.

> I have cut off nations; their battlements are in ruins; I have laid waste their streets so that no one walks in them; their cities have been made desolate, without a man, without an inhabitant. I said, "Surely you will fear Me; you will accept correction. Then your dwelling would not be cut off according to all that I have appointed against you. But all the more they were eager to make all their deeds corrupt. Therefore wait for Me," declares the Lord, "for the day when I rise up to seize the prey. For My decision is to gather nations, to assemble kingdoms, to pour out upon them My indignation, all My burning anger; for in the fire of My jealousy all the earth shall be consumed."

We see the wickedness and sinfulness of men along with the just response of God to vindicate His great name. The city, defiled and oppressive, has become polluted through sins of idolatry and covenant breaking. Rather than showing care and compassion, the city has become a brutal and overbearing place especially for vulnerable people. Leaders, rather than guarding their flock, devour it.

Religious officials are also condemned, including the priests and the prophets. Rather than being speakers of God's sure Word, they speak their own fickle words and defame the offerings of God's people. God calls the city to fear, in respectful awe, at His power. His justice will avenge the pollution of sin. He alone is righteous and holy.

The scene that Zephaniah describes is the scene upon which Jesus will appear—a world sickened by sin and its effects, and a world longing and needing a Savior.

It is because of sin that we have the fatherless. The brokenness of sin results in outcasts. Sin is the author of death. Our rebellion has ushered in a society where children are neglected, abandoned, and lost.

This first section of Zephaniah reveals to us that there is no hope without the Lord's intervention, but as we keep reading, we see the Lord will and does intervene. Zephaniah 3:9-13,

> *For at that time I will change the speech of the peoples to a pure speech, that all of them may call upon the name of the Lord and serve Him with one accord. From beyond the rivers of Cush My worshippers, the daughter of My dispersed ones, shall bring my offering.*

> *On that day you shall not be put to shame because of the deeds by which you have rebelled against Me; for then I will remove from your midst your proudly exultant ones, and you shall no longer be haughty in My holy mountain. But I will leave in your midst a people humble and lowly. They shall seek refuge in the name of the Lord, those who are left in Israel; they shall do no injustice and speak no lies, nor shall there be found in their mouth a deceitful tongue. For they shall graze and lie down, and none shall make them afraid.*

How glorious to see that this loving conversion is not just for Israel, but also for the nations? God will turn our speech from condemnation to praise; from confusing banter to a concatenation of worship. At the tower of Babel, the Lord confused the language because people were trying to band together to exalt themselves. In Zephaniah, we see that the Spirit of God will undo the curse of Babel and unite our speech for His glory and renown. He is exalted through the rejoining of all peoples.

The preaching of the gospel teaches people to use the language of humility, repentance, and faith. By His grace the Lord will shut out boasting and leave men nothing else to glory in, but Jesus the King. Caring for the fatherless is an opportunity to proclaim the gospel alongside tangible action. God will choose for Himself a people who are humble and meek who seek nothing but the name of Christ and His service. How captivating to know that God restores His people, and that He has redeemed us. Not only has He redeemed us for ourselves, but also, He has redeemed us to care for the least of these for His glory.

Zephaniah 3:14-20 finishes this way:

> Sing aloud, O daughter of Zion; shout, O Israel!
> Rejoice and exult with all your heart, O daughter of Jerusalem!
> The Lord has taken away the judgments against you;
> He has cleared away your enemies.
> The King of Israel, the Lord, is in your midst;
> you shall never again fear evil.
>
> On that day it shall be said to Jerusalem:
> "Fear not, O Zion; let not your hands grow weak.
> The Lord your God is in your midst,
> a mighty one who will save;
> He will rejoice over you with gladness;
> He will quiet you by His love;
> He will exult over you with loud singing.
> I will gather those of you who mourn for the festival,
> so that you will no longer suffer reproach.
>
> Behold, at that time I will deal with all your oppressors.
> And I will save the lame and gather the outcast,

and I will change their shame into praise
and renown in all the earth.

At that time I will bring you in,
at the time when I gather you together;
for I will make you renowned and praised
among all the peoples of the earth,
when I restore your fortunes before your eyes," says the Lord.

What a radiant picture of the restoration and redemption of the gospel of Christ. The Lord has taken away His judgments against us and given us His presence and support.

As in the Psalms, people even in the throes of suffering are called to worship and give thanks for their anticipated salvation. Rejoicing is appropriate because of the presence of the real King of Israel, Immanuel, among His people. The human kings of Israel and Judah served only as representatives of Israel's true King. Our King's presence is a blessing to those who repent and return to Him. God's people, who had been far-flung, will face restoration at the hand of their King. Instead of being justifiably shamed for our sin, we are renowned and praised because of the gracious salvation of God.

This gospel is for the meek who will in turn take the gospel to the least of these, including the fatherless. The gospel of King Jesus invites us, beckons us, and commands us to join in the Father's plan to restore the least of these — single moms who are living without the support of a husband and protector; children who are orphaned and living in institutions or on the streets; parents who are living through the generational sin and curse of drugs and abuse or who neglect their children; and children around the world who have been orphaned because of physical, emotional, or social reasons.

Beloved, we have been called to manifest the gospel to them. Are we concerned for the fatherless as God's covenant people? Are we thirsty for the righteousness of Christ? Are we passionate to show the gospel and share the gospel with our neighbors and the nations? Will we ignore the first half of James 1:27 or will we live out pure, faultless and true religion?

Image Bearers - The Children of God

We see in the Old Testament that the people of God were fatherless and yet the Lord makes them a family through Abraham. They were strangers and He gives them a land. They were without a husband and the Lord becomes their husband.

The theology of adoption and the mandate to care for the fatherless continues throughout the New Testament. We see that we were fatherless, and the Lord adopts us through the gospel of Christ. We were strangers, and God gives us His presence and a home through Jesus. We who were once widows become the very Bride of Christ.

Before we can begin serving the fatherless, we must understand our position without Christ and that the gospel is a picture of adoption and the mercy of God.

We are all made in the image of God. The mystery, however, is that in Christ, through His gospel, has given us the right to become sons and daughters of God. This is exactly what you are today if you are a Christ follower. We are the children of God and thus, we must protect and defend life because life is valuable.

Sinclair Ferguson, Scottish theologian and professor at Reformed Theological Seminary says, "The notion that we are children of God, His own sons and daughters...is the mainspring of Christian living....Our sonship to God is the apex of creation and the goal of our redemption."

If we want to understand the essence of being Christian and why being a Christian is a privilege, we need to appreciate divine adoption. We earn the seed and promise of Abraham through adoption. We are his heirs, heirs of the promise through our adoption papers sealed by Christ. This is what fuels our stance for the sanctity of life, racial reconciliation and defending the orphan and widow.

Romans 8:12-17 says,

> So then, brothers, we are debtors, not to the flesh, to live according
> to the flesh. For if you live according to the flesh you will die, but if
> by the Spirit you put to death the deeds of the body, you will live. For
> all who are led by the Spirit of God are sons of God. For you did not
> receive the spirit of slavery to fall back into fear, but you have received
> the Spirit of adoption as sons, by whom we cry, "Abba! Father!" The
> Spirit Himself bears witness with our spirit that we are children of God,
> and if children, then heirs — heirs of God and fellow heirs with Christ,
> provided we suffer with Him in order that we may also be glorified
> with Him.

We see from this passage that ultimately it is the Holy Spirit who confirms that
we are a child of God. The Holy Spirit leads us to hate and war with sin. By the
Holy Spirit's power, the children of God are warring against sin and putting to
death the sinful deeds of the flesh. Personal in nature, the Holy Spirit convicts
us to look inwardly at our own sin. Yes, we hate sin's destruction in the world,
but first, we are to be grieved, convicted, and to repent of the sin that has
contaminated us personally.

Like David in Psalm 51, the Holy Spirit leads us to cry out for mercy. We see
David's cry in verses 1-3:

> Have mercy on me, O God, according to Your steadfast love; according
> to Your abundant mercy blot out my transgressions. Wash me thor-
> oughly from my iniquity, and cleanse me from my sin! For I know my
> transgressions, and my sin is ever before me.

Before we can hate the sin of the world that has left children vulnerable and
orphaned, we must be led by the Spirit to consistently wage war with our old
orphaned spirit as we recognize that in Christ and through His gospel, He
has given us not a spirit of slavery or servitude, but the right to be called His
children.

When we care for orphans and vulnerable children, they will constantly push
back against our efforts to love. They have been deeply hurt and neglected. As

a result, they commonly retreat into themselves. Likewise we have that same orphan spirit, a spirit of sin. But the Holy Spirit gives us assurance of our adoption by leading us to hate and war against sin.

Moreover, the Holy Spirit seals our adoption as sons and leads us to cry out "Abba Father." We have intimacy as we are given the word "Abba"—a term used by babies—which gives us assurance of the love of God. A healthy baby doesn't ever doubt or question the love of his parents.

Additionally, we have been assigned the rights, position, and benefits of only sons of the Father. He sees us as He sees Jesus. Therefore, we do not rely on our works to earn God's favor, but we rest in the sonship which is ours through the atoning life of Christ. We work because we have a deep affection for the Father who He has lavishly loved us.

John Piper says this about the word "Abba":

> These words are not a cheap, computer-like production; rather, the Holy Spirit Himself speaks through us. The Apostle Paul's choice of the Aramaic word Abba indicates that our cry will be sweet, tender, and intimate, and his choice of the word cry shows emotional depth and sincerity — an earnest longing for our Father.

Just like children need and long for the attention of their parents, the Holy Spirit gives us the ability to cry out, and not just to cry out, but the ability to be heard and to be answered. "Cry" means krazdon or a loud cry full of passion and feeling. Specifically, this is a child crying out for their parents. If you are a parent, think about this: Why do your children cry out, "Mommy, Daddy" in the middle of the night? Our children cry out, because they know that we will listen and respond. Orphans and the vulnerable many times have no one to cry out to, but as the Church, we need to wrap around them and be available just like our Father does for us.

Do you know what the most deafening sound is to hear in an orphanage?— Silence. The first time my wife, Ashley, and I travelled to China in 2004, we had the opportunity to visit many crowded orphanages. Upon entering a room full of babies, you would think it would be very loud. It was actually quite the opposite. Hundreds of babies in one room and not one of them making a sound.

I have heard from many families who bring their children home through adoption that they are astonished when their newly adopted kids fall, scrape their knees, and make no cries at all. Why do you think they don't cry? Because these precious image bearers don't know what it is like to have their cries answered. We have a Heavenly Father who hears us when we call or cry out to Him.

Beloved, if you are a child of God today, you have the ability and the privilege to cry out to your Father and to cry out to Him on behalf of those with no earthly father. When life is hard, cry out to Him because He will listen. Brother and sister, cry out to God because He hears His children. When the journey you are on is tough, cry out. The Holy Spirit seals our adoption as sons and daughters and leads us to cry out "Abba Father." Not only do we have an intimacy with the Father because of our adoption, but in Christ, we are granted assurance by the Holy Spirit who gives us confidence and boldness as heirs of God even as we suffer with Christ.

The journey of adoption and orphan care are difficult and can involve immense suffering. When you enter into the world of the orphan and the vulnerable child, you are entering into their suffering and their sorrow and making it your own. When you show love, many times they do not know how to receive that love and will war against it. We cannot be fooled into thinking that the call to care for orphans is a call to comfort. My friend Russell Moore says, "adoption and orphan care are spiritual warfare."

We are true heirs of God if we suffer with Him. This conditional phrase certainly does not mean that we seek persecution like a Japanese kamikaze pilot. Rather we suffer because sin has marred the glorious and perfect creation of our Father. We suffer because we no longer associate our lives with this fallen

We are true heirs of God if we suffer with Him.

world, but with the remaking of God's coming Kingdom on earth. You can know that you are a child of God when this world no longer feels like home, and your thoughts are captured with the eternal presence of your Father God.

Romans 8:18-21 explains it this way:

> For I consider that the sufferings of this present time are not worth comparing with the glory that is to be revealed to us. For the creation waits with eager longing for the revealing of the sons of God. For the creation was subjected to futility, not willingly, but because of him who subjected it, in hope that the creation itself will be set free from its bondage to corruption and obtain the freedom of the glory of the children of God.

Beloved, this is our hope if we are children of God — hope that creation will be restored, hope that our Father will come and reign and that we will be with Him forever.

Why is our inheritance tied to suffering? At least in part, because if we as fallen people do not face trials, we will become so consumed with ourselves and our lives that we forget about God. God's allowance of suffering is different for all of His children, but when we suffer, let us not shake our fists at His face. Instead, let us say, "Father, use this light and momentary suffering for Your good, Your glory, and the spread of Your gospel." I am not saying that this will be an easy thing to do. When suffering has come to my own life, I have had to remind myself of the truth of Scripture to be able to make it through each day. We will suffer, but as we suffer, we must choose to cling to the hope of Jesus. We are sanctified by our confidence that all of our suffering is designed to help us lean wholly on Him.

2 Corinthians 4:16-18 reminds us:

> So we do not lose heart. Though our outer self is wasting away, our inner self is being renewed day by day. For this light, momentary affliction is preparing for us an eternal weight of glory beyond all comparison, as we look not to the things that are seen but to the things

that are unseen. For the things that are seen are transient, but the
things that are unseen are eternal.

Beloved, as the legitimate children of God we are called by God to spread His
gospel and many times to do so by our acts of gospel-driven justice. Caring
for orphans, the poor, the needy, the vulnerable, and the least of these is not
always easy. In fact, at times it may cost us our comfort, our "peace," or our
earthly security. Know this: our great God will give us boldness, courage, and
conviction as we defend the fatherless and embrace those in need.

Responding to the call of the gospel on our lives should give us great courage
and effective witness to follow the commands and examples of Jesus even
against the face of great adversity. Our Lord has called us to be counter-
cultural as we defend the sanctity of life, as we embrace our racial and ethnic
differences as imprints of the *Imago Dei*, and as we seek justice for the
defenseless, the orphan, widow, poor, and needy. Rest assured that the
same God who calls us will equip us and grant us great courage to carry out
this work.

Not only do we see the ways that the Holy Spirit confirms that we are the
children of God, we also see the benefits of being children of God from
Romans 8:12-17.

The first benefit we see is acceptance by God. We have been chosen in
adoption as sons of God (v. 15). The message of the gospel tells us who we
really are. We are weak, dirty, and messy fools. This message is humbling
because over and over again it reminds me that I am in a hopeless,
impossible, and irreversible state apart from divine intervention.

> *But God, being rich in mercy, because of the great love with which*
> *He loved us, even when we were dead in our trespasses, made*
> *us alive together with Christ — by grace you have been saved.*
> —**Ephesians 2:4-5**

The fatherless can't do anything to be accepted. There is nothing they can do
to find a family or support. They are dependent. Oh beloved sinner, this is the

good news of spiritual adoption. Just like an orphaned child, trapped, lonely, and possessing nothing to be noticed, God pursues you with His adopting love and accepts you out of His great love. You are no longer unacceptable, but now, a child of God, fully accepted by Him because of the work of Jesus on the cross.

We are those fatherless children. Our great God is that adoptive daddy who accepts us, not on our merit but on His. And through that merit, the Lord doesn't just accept us, but He transforms our identity into that of Christ. We begin to imitate Christ once our adoption papers are sealed through our salvation. We are given the Holy Spirit who enables us to become more Christlike. We have moment by moment dependence and relationship.

> *Therefore, if anyone is in Christ, he is a new creation. The old has passed away; behold, the new has come.* —**2 Corinthians 5:17**

One of the benefits of homeschooling our children is that we have the opportunity to do science experiments at home. To display the wonder of creation and metamorphosis, Ashley ordered several caterpillars. The kids could not wait for the day these caterpillars would be delivered via the US mail. It was a spellbinding several weeks as we watched tiny caterpillars be transformed into a new creation of a butterfly. Out of the cocoon of death came the rebirth into a beautiful butterfly.

In the same way, our identity has been exchanged. We are no longer seen as sinners, but as righteous just as Christ is righteous. Through the power of the gospel and adoption, God is changing our primary identity. We see Him changing identities of His people throughout the Bible. For example, barren Abram becomes Abraham, the father of a multitude. Simon, who was a self-reliant, brash, denier of Christ, becomes Peter, the rock on which Christ would plant His Church. And Saul the persecutor of Christians, becomes Paul, the greatest evangelist the world has known.

Our adoption in Christ also gives us a new identity in Christ and a new name, because through our adoption we gain belonging in the family of God. We are now one in Christ. We have more in common with the family of God than we do with biological family members who do not know Christ. There is a kinship with fellow believers as we join together, live together, and worship our Father together. We have more in common with the believer living in rural Africa, than our next door neighbor who rejects Christ.

Some of my closest relationships are with people around the world who look very different from me. I have mentioned my dear brother Pastor Raphael, and time and space fail me to expound on the deep relationships that Christ has forged between me and brothers around the world like Sasha, Krupa, Rufus, Isaac, and so many more. Through the gospel, adoption tears down barriers of race and culture, class and socioeconomic level, to create a multi-cultural, multi-ethnic, and diverse family that bears the image of their Creator. We are not slaves; we are sons.

Beloved, you can have assurance that you are indeed a child of God. The reality of our adoption changes our perspective on how we operate. Our God is great, He owns it all, and He is in control. No matter the circumstances, this should give us great courage. Therefore, we follow Him in caring for the fatherless, in taking the gospel to our neighbors, in loving the poor and needy, in gospel reconciliation, and in protecting the value of human life.

Practical Ways to Care for the Fatherless

God gives His adoptive children a mandate to care for the fatherless, but He doesn't leave us without a beautiful application on how to do this. He gives us this grand application through the book of Ruth. Beyond the discussion in Chapter 7, I want to tease out some practical lessons from this rich story to inform our orphan care activities.

Ruth is a widow, a stranger, an alien, and an orphan. Her vulnerability is compounded by each of these identities, and we can learn a great deal from how God meets her needs through His people. Looking at Ruth Chapter 1, we can gather some powerful context for our understanding.

We learn that an Israelite man named Elimelech takes his wife, Naomi, and his two sons from Israel to live among Moabites. A famine was ravishing the land of Israel, Elimelech takes matters into his own hands, and out of desperation moves into this enemy territory. To put it lightly, the Moabites and Israelites were fierce enemies and shared the current resentment of India and Pakistan.

While in Moab, Elimelech leads his sons to disobey the commandment of God to not intermarry with those of other faiths. Both sons married Moabite women, Orpah and Ruth. However, in short order, all of the men die and Naomi, Ruth, and Orpah are left as widows.

Naomi, knowing she has nothing to offer her daughters-in-law, orders them to return to their families because she is returning to Israel; however, Ruth has now committed herself to the God of Israel and to her mother-in-law. Ruth pledges her loyalty to Naomi in Ruth 1:16: *"But Ruth said, 'Do not urge me to leave you or to return from following you. For where you go I will go, and where you lodge I will lodge. Your people shall be my people, and your God my God.'"*

Don't miss the context of this passage that is quoted so many times in wedding ceremonies. This is not a man or woman pledging themselves to a wife or husband, but a daughter-in-law pledging herself to her mother-in-law. This is radical.

Because of this radical abandon with which Ruth pledges herself she now represents the three vulnerable groups echoed throughout the Bible. She is a widow from losing her husband. She is a stranger/alien as she enters into enemy lands away from her citizenship in Moab. And practically, because she has left Moab and devoted herself to another God and people, she is functionally an orphan. This is the scene that precedes Ruth Chapter 2. In this chapter we see beautiful application of how to care for widows, strangers, and the fatherless. Remember as you read Ruth Chapter 2 that the story is told by a narrator. As a result, we are seeing things that Ruth doesn't yet see or know.

In Ruth 2 we read,

> Now Naomi had a relative of her husband's, a worthy man of the clan of Elimelech, whose name was Boaz. And Ruth the Moabite said to Naomi, "Let me go to the field and glean among the ears of grain after him in whose sight I shall find favor." And she said to her, "Go, my daughter." So she set out and went and gleaned in the field after the reapers, and she happened to come to the part of the field belonging to Boaz, who was of the clan of Elimelech. And behold, Boaz came from Bethlehem. And he said to the reapers, "The Lord be with you!" And they answered, "The Lord bless you." Then Boaz said to a young man who was in charge of the reapers, "Whose young woman is this?" And the servant who was in charge of the reapers answered, "She is the young Moabite woman, who came back with Naomi from the country of Moab." She said, "Please let me glean and gather among the sheaves after the reapers." So she came, and she has continued from early morning until now, except for a short rest."

> Then Boaz said to Ruth, "Now, listen, my daughter, do not go to glean in another field or leave this one, but keep close to my young women. Let your eyes be on the field that they are reaping, and go after them. Have I not charged the young men not to touch you? And when you are thirsty, go to the vessels and drink what the young men have drawn." Then she fell on her face, bowing to the ground, and said to him, "Why have I found favor in your eyes, that you should take notice of me, since I am a foreigner?" But Boaz answered her, "All that you have done for your mother-in-law since the death of your husband has been fully told to me, and how you left your father and mother and your native land and came to a people that you did not know before. The Lord repay you for what you have done, and a full reward be given you by the Lord, the God of Israel, under whose wings you have come to take refuge!" Then she said, "I have found favor in your eyes, my lord, for you have comforted me and spoken kindly to your servant, though I am not one of your servants."

And at mealtime Boaz said to her, "Come here and eat some bread and dip your morsel in the wine." So she sat beside the reapers, and he passed to her roasted grain. And she ate until she was satisfied, and she had some left over. When she rose to glean, Boaz instructed his young men, saying, "Let her glean even among the sheaves, and do not reproach her. And also pull out some from the bundles for her and leave it for her to glean, and do not rebuke her."

So she gleaned in the field until evening. Then she beat out what she had gleaned, and it was about an ephah of barley. And she took it up and went into the city. Her mother-in-law saw what she had gleaned. She also brought out and gave her what food she had left over after being satisfied. And her mother-in-law said to her, "Where did you glean today? And where have you worked? Blessed be the man who took notice of you." So she told her mother-in-law with whom she had worked and said, "The man's name with whom I worked today is Boaz." And Naomi said to her daughter-in-law, "May he be blessed by the Lord, whose kindness has not forsaken the living or the dead!" Naomi also said to her, "The man is a close relative of ours, one of our redeemers." And Ruth the Moabite said, "Besides, he said to me, 'You shall keep close by my young men until they have finished all my harvest.'"

And Naomi said to Ruth, her daughter-in-law, "It is good, my daughter, that you go out with his young women, lest in another field you be assaulted." So she kept close to the young women of Boaz, gleaning until the end of the barley and wheat harvests. And she lived with her mother-in-law.

Here we see that Boaz is a kinsman-redeemer of Ruth and Naomi. The kinsman-redeemer was a male relative who, according to the Law given to Israel by God, had the privilege and responsibility to act on behalf of a relative who was in danger or need. In God's great providence, Ruth had not wandered onto a random field, but the field of a man who feared God and followed the commands of God we saw earlier in Deuteronomy 24.

In this passage we see six distinct ways that **Boaz cares for Ruth and thus a pattern for caring for the fatherless.** Boaz sees Ruth's value and sees past her vulnerability. He doesn't just show charity to her but is intimate, loving and kind. Boaz cherishes Ruth as an image bearer and serves as a model for us.

First, we see that **Boaz takes notice of Ruth.** He comes back from his trip and approaches her with kindness, keeping his eye on her to make sure she is being treated fairly. Boaz doesn't avoid making contact, but enters into Ruth's world. We also must take notice of the fatherless, just as the Lord took notice of us. While we were yet sinners and outcast, Christ died for us.

> *For while we were still weak, at the right time Christ died for the ungodly. For one will scarcely die for a righteous person — though perhaps for a good person one would dare even to die but God shows His love for us in that while we were still sinners, Christ died for us.*
> —**Romans 5:6-8**

Because we of all people should know what it feels like for the God of the universe to take notice, in turn, we take notice of the fatherless.

Second, **Boaz provides for Ruth's needs including food, shelter, clothing, and essentials.** Also, we see from the passage that this is not a one time showering of help which then leads to apathy, but a continuation of meeting needs. Boaz instructs his young men to allow her to take whatever she needs and to even leave out more for her to glean.

Are we making our fields available in the same way for the fatherless, the way that our Father has so richly provided for us? Do we respond reluctantly to the needs of the fatherless or do we seek to continually meet needs? We see in Matthew 6:25-34 that the Lord knows and provides for all of our essential needs on a continual basis. This is why the Lord tells us not to be anxious about tomorrow.

Third, **Boaz affirms and blesses Ruth.** He continually speaks words of kindness. The fatherless and their mothers live in a world of pain and rejection with the great fear of further loss. Boaz spoke affectionately and kindly to remind Ruth of her value to God. When we do this for others, it is like pouring rain on parched ground. God spoke His kind words of redemption to us and wooed us while we were far away.

> See what kind of love the Father has given to us, that we should be called children of God; and so we are. The reason why the world does not know us is that it did not know Him. Beloved, we are God's children now, and what we will be has not yet appeared; but we know that when He appears we shall be like Him, because we shall see Him as He is. —1 John 3:1-12

Fourth, we observe how **Boaz protects Ruth and advocates for her safety making her a priority, not a burden.** With his young men, he sets up plans for her ongoing protection.

In the same way, let us not be burdened by the commands of God, but joyfully serve and protect the fatherless. In the same way that Jesus joyfully protects us from the wrath deserved because of our sin, we must advocate for them and for their safety.

> Therefore, since we are surrounded by so great a cloud of witnesses, let us also lay aside every weight, and sin which clings so closely, and let us run with endurance the race that is set before us, looking to Jesus, the founder and perfecter of our faith, who for the joy that was set before Him endured the cross, despising the shame, and is seated at the right hand of the throne of God. Consider Him who endured from sinners such hostility against Himself, so that you may not grow weary or fainthearted. In your struggle against sin you have not yet resisted to the point of shedding your blood. —Hebrews 12:1-4

Fifth, **Boaz honors Ruth and brings her in to sit at his table with him.** During this time, meals were intimate times of relationship, not utilitarian as they are today in the West. As an act of intimacy, not charity, Boaz honors Ruth by inviting her into his home to sit at his table.

In the same manner, let us love, honor, bless and invite the fatherless to our table. We do this in the same way that Jesus came to earth to seek and save the lost and to ultimately invite us in to dine with Him. Luke 19:10 says, *"For the Son of Man came to seek and to save the lost."* And we see in the Song of Solomon 2:4 that *"He brought me to the banqueting table, and His banner over me is love."*

Lastly and undeniably, we see **Boaz redeems Ruth by inviting her into his family.** He makes her a citizen, a wife, and a child of a family. We see this all recorded in Ruth 4 and learn that Ruth's children would be in the line of King David and ultimately the lineage of the long awaited Messiah. After a PG-13 scene in Ruth 2, we see in Ruth 4 that Boaz proceeds to the city center and makes it known that he desires to redeem Ruth, to marry her, and bring her into his family. The adoptive love Boaz has for Ruth mirrors the adoptive love our Heavenly Father has for us!

Ultimately, we know that the defender of the fatherless is the Lord. We rest knowing that the hope of the oppressed, fatherless, and the widow is not in us, but in the Lord. Psalm 68:5-6 says, *"God is the Father of the fatherless and protector of widows. He settles the solitary in a family and leads out the neglected to prosperity."*

We see that while the Book of Ruth offers plentiful practical insight into the way we care for the fatherless, it equally serves to foreshadow the mercy, grace, justice and love which flows from the ultimate kinsman-redeemer, Jesus. When we participate in the mercy of the justice of the Kingdom, then we are showing and displaying the glory of God.

Isaiah 58:9-11 says,

> *Then you shall call, and the Lord will answer; you shall cry, and He will say, "Here I am." If you take away the yoke from your midst, the point-ing of the finger, and speaking wickedness, if you pour yourself out for the hungry and satisfy the desire of the afflicted, then shall your light rise in the darkness and your gloom be as the noonday. And the Lord will guide you continually and satisfy your desire in scorched places*

*and make your bones strong; and you shall be like a watered garden,
like a spring of water, whose waters do not fail.*

Ministry to the fatherless has consistently been the way of the Church. Unfortunately, today we are allowing the government and secular non-governmental organizations to attempt to perform the job given to the Church.

In A.D. 125 Aristides, an Athenian statesman, said about the Church,

*They do not worship strange gods, and they go their way in all
modesty and cheerfulness. Falsehood is not found among them; and
they love one another, and from widows they do not turn away their
esteem; and they deliver the orphan from him who treats him harshly.
And he, who has, gives to him who has not, without boasting.*

Beloved, we cannot truly say we are pro-life if we abandon our God-given role to care for the fatherless. When we fail to intervene on behalf of the fatherless, we are showing a secular and dying world that we are more interested in birth than life. On the contrary, the gospel of Christ shows believers that we are not the rescuers of these children—we are the rescued. We have so lavishly been loved by Christ in our despair and rescued from our sin. As a result we are compelled to care for the orphan, the widow, the poor, the needy, and the alien.

So why did we, the Church as God's people, stop caring for the vulnerable? I believe there are many plausible reasons. First, it was **the lack of voice of the fatherless.** We live in such a distracted time and age. The technology age has certainly brought many blessings of convenience and efficiency, but it has also ushered in an age of seclusion and busyness. We fill our calendars with activity, but ultimately live in a world of obscurity. The fatherless have no voice and no standing. As a result, they are vulnerable. When the Church isn't aggressively and actively seeking gospel-driven justice, it makes it a lot more sanitary to avoid and ignore the injustice around us.

Another reason the Church stopped caring for the fatherless is **government intervention on a broad scale.** When the church became preoccupied and stopped seeking to do justice for the fatherless, the government stepped in and filled the void, realizing that there was a major social problem that must be addressed. In almost every country in the world you will find orphanages and organizations which are serving the fatherless from a Christian background; however, many of these are now relics of the old or have been taken over by the government.

We cannot resent the government for stepping in, but we must mourn that we turned a blind eye. If the Church wants to reinsert itself around the world, it must first serve the system in humility. Also, we must pray for government workers and ask the Lord for avenues to re-engage the system with opportunities to intervene. We must remember that it is much easier to lose a responsibility than to regain it.

Furthermore, the Church stopped caring for the fatherless because of a **weak theology which led to a "prosperity theology."** The prosperity theology states that you can live your best life now and that following Jesus means physical blessing and comfort. It is antithetical to the prosperity gospel to serve the fatherless and vulnerable. Contrary to a life of ease and comfort, many adoptive and foster parents will tell you stories of heartache, heartbreak, difficulty, sleepless nights, and thoughts of hopelessness.

The vulnerable, stranger, and fatherless all live in darkness, and so when we take the light of the gospel to them we can expect that the adversary will counterattack. And these attacks are harsh. You see, the fatherless live in a world of all types of pain, trauma, abuse, and neglect. When we enter into their world, we are bringing their hurt and pain into our lives.

This pain is uncomfortable and it certainly is incongruent to a theology that says that in Christ there is only blessing and prosperity. If we are living only for comfort and blessing in this world then we will naturally avoid things that are difficult and heartbreaking. The prosperity theology/gospel is in stark conflict with caring for the fatherless.

The true biblical gospel of the Lord Jesus Christ; however, is not in conflict with our mission to care for the fatherless. As a matter of fact, the gospel is the very reason that we care for orphans.

We cannot ignore the physically poor and downtrodden around us. We cannot fall into these mistakes, but must be people who are vigilant about preaching the gospel to the spiritually bankrupt, as well as showing the gospel to the physically poor. Our theology will affect our biography. What we believe about God will affect the way we act, live, and worship.

Theologian A.W. Tozer said, "The most important thing about you is what you think about God."

We don't have a shortage today on teaching the Word, especially in the U.S., but we do have a shortage of application and mobilization. We need not only talk the talk, but begin walking out justice for the physically and socially poor. Doing orphan care and other forms of justice is about reflecting the very heart of the gospel, and we do it to honor and reflect the glory of God which has come to redeem us.

Bible teacher and author Kay Arthur of Precept Ministries International defines the call to reflect the glory of God in such a profound way. She says, "We are to live in such a way as to give all of creation a correct opinion or estimate of who God is."

The Apostle Paul says it this way to the church at Corinth in 2 Corinthians 5:20: *"Therefore, we are ambassadors for Christ, God making His appeal through us. We implore you on behalf of Christ, be reconciled to God."*

So beloved, we are called to join the work of the Lord in bringing liberty to the captives, healing to the sick and blind, and bringing validation to the fatherless. The gospel shows us who we really are. Our adoption is not based on the fact that we were cute, attractive, or worthy, but it is based on the sovereign grace of God set out before the beginning of the world. Our adoption is based on the fact that He is worthy.

Friend in Christ, you have a Father who is pursuing you and marked you out before the foundation of the world. Just as in physical adoption and orphan care, there is nothing a child can do to be chosen or to advocate for themselves. They need the right person, with the right pedigree, and the right resources to look after them. We have the Author, Sustainer, and Creator of the universe who has sought after our souls. He is most assuredly the right one with perfect pedigree and unlimited resources.

These facts propel us to engage in defending the fatherless. But, practically speaking, how can our churches begin ministering to the fatherless?

1. We can minister through adoption ministry which involves assisting families explore adoption; helping families fund adoption; and supporting families before, during, and after the adoption.

2. We can participate in foster care ministry which includes recruiting and training foster families; recruiting and training respite families; and caring for families who take foster care placements by prayer, acts of service, and reminding them the promises of God. We can begin to minister to workers in the government system, the government, and non-believing foster families.

3. We can also begin participating in strategic orphan care. This includes ministering to caregivers in institutions; minimizing developmental deficits by utilizing tutoring programs, education programs, and therapy; teaching and mentoring older orphans with job and life skills; helping with transitional assistance for older orphans who are aging out; and developing programs for reunification of orphans into their biological families through gospel intervention.

4. Ministry to the fatherless also looks like getting engaged with birthparent and reunification ministry. We bring the gospel to bear in the family of origin when we help families who are struggling and at risk of losing their kids by teaching about biblical family and parenting. We should always seek reunification and not focus all of our attention on the fatherless while ignoring their families of origin.

Equally important, we need to make caring for the fatherless a regular focus of preaching. Every November the global church participates in an initiative called "Orphan Sunday," on the second Sunday of the month. Our churches need to participate in Orphan Sunday or set aside another regular time to preach about gospel-driven justice for the fatherless. Lifeline is excited to provide resources each year including videos, Bible study lessons, and other materials to help your church with Orphan Sunday. Please visit www.lifelinechild.org/orphan-sunday to get your free resources.

Beloved, we all are called to care. We are all commanded to use our lives to engage with the marginalized and the fatherless. So the question is, following the commands of the Bible, what will we do? We must remember that James 1:27 is a call not only to adoption, but a call to be continually engaged with the orphan.

(un)adopted – When Adoption Isn't Possible

In 2008, on a trip to Zaporizhia, Ukraine, the Lord awoke my heart to the fact that adoption alone could not answer the cry of the orphan. It was in Ukraine that I first met a young girl named Kataya; she was reportedly 15 and desperately wanted a family. Kataya's younger sisters had been adopted when she was eight years old; however, the adoptive family decided they did not want to adopt an eight year old because that was just "too old." So instead, they split the family apart leaving Kataya behind in the orphanage.

It became my personal mission to right this wrong and quickly find Kataya a family as she was swiftly approaching her 16th birthday. Once Kataya reached the age of 16 she would no longer be eligible to receive an adoption visa from the U.S. government.

Depending on the source, there are an estimated 153 million orphans around the world like Kataya. The term "orphan" as a descriptor can be misleading — traditionally defined as a child deprived of one or both parents by death. However, today the definition of an orphan has become much more expansive. Many of the worldwide "orphans" are social orphans, deprived of family because of abuse, poverty, special need, or even governmental restriction.

No matter how one chooses to define the word "orphan," the truth remains that there are 153 million orphaned or vulnerable children in our world. This is an epidemic to which adoption alone cannot and should not be the only answer. Other options must be pursued to prevent families from abandoning their children either by choice, force, or despair. Our single motivation should not be to only to help those children who are adoptable, healthy, young, and culturally acceptable; but instead, to reach out to the broken, the hurting, the sick, the poor, the needy, the culturally unacceptable, and to the (un)adoptable.

Upon returning to the U.S. from Ukraine, Lifeline staff began a full-fledged effort desperately searching for a family who would consider adopting Kataya. Information was spread through all known outlets until finally an exceptional family came to the forefront. With great urgency our stateside team quickly called Ukraine and informed them of the news. Because this was an unorthodox match, we had not yet secured Kataya's paperwork. It would only be a matter of time until her papers were in hand and the process would begin.

Two days later Lifeline received a call that changed everything. In the haste to respond to Kataya's needs, our tunnel vision drove us to think only of adoption, and we overlooked one significant detail. This orphanage had two 15-year-olds named Kataya. The orphanage had given us the wrong birthdate — our Kataya had already turned 16; Kataya would remain (un)adopted. We were crushed.

Unfortunately, the truth is that this is the same fate for 99.5% of the world's orphans—*less than one half of one percent* ever find permanence either with their biological families or with adoptive families. We can argue that much more could be done to restore biological families and that more should be done to encourage and equip indigenous adoption; however, this alone does not address the inevitable problem. Without true intervention on a strategic level, many of the world's 153 million "orphans" will find themselves a victim of crime, human trafficking, or suicide, and most certainly impoverished.

At Lifeline we are compelled by the call of Christ in James 1:27 to care for the orphan and widow in their distress; therefore, we have embarked on a journey of strategic orphan care through a ministry initiative – (un)adopted®.

(un)adopted seeks to develop a sustainable ministry model that can be replicated throughout the world. The ministry seeks to mobilize the indigenous international Church to care for orphans and the impoverished in their communities with viable long-term solutions, while also exposing American churches, students, and business people to the plight of orphans, the poor and the needy.

(un)adopted currently has projects in many countries, including the country of Uganda. In Uganda, international adoption has been almost eradicated and replaced with an arduous process for both the children and prospective parents. Meanwhile, hundreds of thousands of vulnerable children and street orphans struggle for their existence.

Many Ugandan children are being neglected and abandoned simply because they were born deaf. The country is steeped in superstition with witch doctors who have convinced their people that children born deaf are accursed. They believe that deaf children can bring curses upon their families. Because of this belief and the extravagant cost of mediocre schooling for deaf children, a vast number of deaf children are forced to live on the streets as third class citizens. Still others live with reluctant extended family members or single parents who struggle even to provide the most basic of necessities.

In 2011 we met with our dear brother and friend Pastor Raphael Kajjubi who serves a smaller community outside the capital of Kampala, Uganda. (More of Pastor Raphael's story may be found in Chapter 6). One Saturday afternoon walking the dusty streets of the community, Raphael introduced me to 12 deaf children in his community including Mutebi, Anderson, and Adam.

When we first met Mutebi, he was wallowing in the dirt without dignity or hope. His mother, the community witch doctor, treated him with contempt. She was truly aghast that anyone would take interest in her son. It was abundantly clear that Mutebi had been brutally beaten, and both Pastor and I wondered if he could even walk.

I remember then visiting with Anderson, his sister, and mother. With all their worldly possessions, they lived together in a "house" that was smaller than your guest room walk in closet. When I showed up with my pearly white skin, Anderson yelped with such fear of the ghost set before him that it took 20 minutes for him to be comforted. Anderson's mom couldn't work because he would never leave her side. Then, his mom confided in us that she felt she had no other choice but to abandon Anderson the next day in the bush, because without being able to work, she and her daughter were sure they would starve.

Adam was living with his mom and sister as well. They had been a prominent family in the community until the day that Adam got sick and lost his hearing. His father, a staunch Muslim, left the family assuming that Allah had placed a curse on his family. Adam's mom was faithfully cutting hair in order to provide for her family, but she was worried because Adam lived in a world of isolation, and his sadness was captured all over his countenance.

As we visited these children, a vision was birthed. In coordination, the local church and (un)adopted would provide sign language, education, life skills, job skills, and hope to these precious faces dotting the landscape of the community. Plans were quickly defined and in a brief six weeks, provisions were secured for desks, simple supplies, a TV, blackboard, and a teacher. The church building would house the school during the week.

The ministry instantly caught the attention of the community, because in this Muslim dominated slum, it was completely counter-cultural to care for the deaf, or the "fools" as translated from the local language. However, wonder and curiosity of the community turned into questions and seeking. Not only were people amazed, but they were also being introduced to Jesus. Additionally, Pastor began to learn that deaf children abound in large numbers throughout the community. There was abundantly more need than King Jesus Church could ever meet. It was during these years that we met Angela and Precious. Angela, who is deaf, had been brutally raped repeatedly to the point that she became pregnant and gave birth to Precious - blind at birth.

Now, eight years later, the school is a centerpiece of the community. Families are restored through love poured out for their formerly "cursed" children. Hope is restored for children who were once deemed hopeless. Skills are taught through an Internet café, brick-making facility, and sewing center, all of which were built to help sustain the school and provide enrichment for the children. Change is being seen as Mutebi walks with confidence, Adam's smile lights up the room, and Anderson embraces friendships with peers he never knew before. Today, this project in a nondescript village in Uganda is accomplishing the mission of (un)adopted by transforming a community of disenfranchised orphans and abandoned children.

Our prayer is that adoptive parents who have provided a home to an orphan through international adoption would continue to invest in their adopted children's country of origin. We also trust that the global Church will begin to care for orphans, not only through adoption, but ultimately by giving of their time, talent, and resources to care strategically for those who are left (un)adopted.

Adoption and Orphan Care Take Perseverance

Put not your trust in princes, in a son of man, in whom there is no salvation. When his breath departs, he returns to the earth; on that very day his plans perish. —**Psalm 146:3-4**

The psalmist is cautioning us strongly against putting any confidence in man. In a culture that exalts those who are rich and famous, athletes, leaders and people verified on Twitter, we must be extremely cautious not to place hope in ourselves on our journey to care for the fatherless.

Pastor and author Paul David Tripp says,

You are tempted to think that because you're God's child, your life should be easier, more predictable, and definitely more comfortable. But that's not what the Bible teaches. Instead, it reveals that struggles are part of God's plan for you. This means that if you're God's child, you must never allow yourself to think that the hard things you are now going through are failures of God's character, promises, power, or plan. You must not allow yourself to think that God has turned His back on you. You must not let yourself begin to buy into the possibility that God is not as trustworthy as you thought Him to be. You must not let yourself do any of these things, because when you begin to doubt God's goodness, you quit going to Him for help. You see, you don't run for help to those characters you have come to doubt. God has chosen to let you live in this fallen world because He plans to employ the difficulties of it to continue and complete His work in you. This means that those moments of difficulty are not an interruption of His plan or the failure of His plan, but rather an important part of His plan.

So adoptive parent, foster parent, or family who is now going through the adoption or foster care process, you have an advocate and His name is Jehovah. We are all called to do justice, but not by ourselves.

I love what George Müller, the German missionary to England's orphans, says: "Faith does not operate in the realm of the possible. There is no glory for God in that which is humanly possible. Faith begins where man's power ends."

Let me illustrate, a year ago, I joined a gym in order to do some strength training. I am one of those people who want a great value. So I joined the gym when there were $0 joining fees, lots of perks, and a free intro period. One of the perks was a personalized workout plan with a physical trainer.

A few weeks after joining I went in for a visit but was told by the trainer, who was an extremely strong man, that I had to pay an additional $150 to get the plan I was expecting. Disappointed I went back to the guy who had processed my enrollment. He told me he would make sure I got my complementary plan and began scheduling another consultation with a trainer.

I had a decision to make. Do I schedule the next consultation with the same trainer or a new trainer? My wise wife said to get a new trainer. This stubborn

husband decided to stay with the same trainer because I didn't want to be "offensive." Well, sweet Ashley was right. The trainer, frustrated that I was back, worked me out to the point that I literally collapsed.

He then thrust me the sheet for my personal plan with a smug grunt. After looking at the full plan, I realized in his frustration the trainer had taken me through an entire weeks worth of workouts in a mere hour and a half. Needless to say, I didn't move well for at least a week.

When we enter into the work of defending the fatherless we may feel like the Lord is throwing everything at us at once, just like the trainer did to me. We may see the work of gospel-driven justice as too hard and messy. But dear Christ-follower, take heart because our precious Savior will strongly support you and be your strength.

Don't forget Romans 11:33-36,

> *Oh, the depth of the riches and wisdom and knowledge of God! How unsearchable are His judgments and how inscrutable His ways! For who has known the mind of the Lord, or who has been His counselor? Or who has given a gift to Him that He might be repaid? For from Him and through Him and to Him are all things. To Him be glory forever. Amen.*

Our great God will strongly support His children as they faithfully follow Him in serving the vulnerable and the fatherless. We must trust in God to supply our needs and to bring encouragement and perseverance to our hearts, minds, and lives. But we must also fight burning out and becoming apathetic. John Piper says,

> *Apathy is passionless living. It is sitting in front of the TV night after night and living your life from one moment of entertainment to the next. It is the inability to be shocked into action by the steady-state lostness and suffering of the world. It is the emptiness that comes from thinking of godliness as the avoidance of doing bad things instead of the aggressive pursuit of doing good things. People who stay at home and watch clean videos don't get persecuted. Godliness must mean something more public, more aggressively good.*

If you are a Christ-follower, then our Lord has called you to be counter-cultural. He has called you to defend the sanctity of life; to embrace racial and ethnic differences as imprints of the *Imago Dei*; and to seek justice for the defenseless, the orphan, widow, poor, and needy.

Trust me, this calling is not the primrose path. This isn't a calling that will bring about earthly prosperity. Instead, this is a life surrendered to the command to build Christ's Kingdom here on earth. Be assured, the same God who calls you, will equip you and grant you great courage and conviction.

Today, our response to the glory of our adoption in Christ cannot be silence. We cannot apathetically sit on the sidelines, because our Father has released us to live with reckless abandon for the high calling to make the gospel known to every tribe, tongue, and people.

Will you get engaged and take responsibility for the 153 million fatherless children in our world? Will you make it your mission to manifest this glorious gospel to the vulnerable and fatherless?

Has the Lord put your family in a place to adopt or foster a precious child in need and, in so doing, disciple them in the gospel of Christ? Has the Lord burdened you with His command in James 1:27 to care for orphans in distress? If so, do not hesitate to get engaged today and begin to defend the fatherless.

Discussion Questions

1. How does scripture inform that it is not the responsibility of the government or the elite to care for children, but it is the command given directly to God's redeemed people?

2. How does the meaning of the word "visit" in James 1:27 influence your understanding of orphan care?

3. It is through our spiritual adoption that the Holy Spirit leads us to hate and war against sin. How is that evident in your personal fight against sin and in the fight for the fatherless?

4. Discuss the hope found in Romans 8:18-21 and how it speaks to the eventual extinction of fatherlessness.

5. Why did we, God's people, stop caring for the vulnerable? How can your church begin a ministry to care for the vulnerable using the people and resources you already have?

Chapter Ten

SLAVERY, TRAFFICKING, AND PORNOGRAPHY

If to be feelingly alive to the sufferings of my fellow-creatures is to be a fanatic, I am one of the most incurable fanatics ever permitted to be at large.

— William Wilberforce, Emancipator of slaves in England

It was one of those calls that takes your breath away. I remember when our receptionist and birthmother counselor first notified me of the situation; I thought the call must have been a prank. The call came quickly from a desperate caller in a hotel room in South Alabama. A young lady who we will call "Betty" told us emphatically that she was being held against her will by ruthless men.

Captured by a group of men, she was held against her will as their prisoner. The owner of the hotel was a part of this scheme, so she begged us to be careful in calling her back for fear her captors might kill her.

Betty's room and the rest of the hotel were being used as a revolving door for men to come in for a price to abuse Betty, take advantage of her, and shame her. Because she remembered our number from years before when we helped her find a family for her first child, she called Lifeline.

Betty knew that she was pregnant and believed that if she couldn't escape her captors, the baby would die. In my mind, I went immediately from Executive Director of an orphan care and adoption ministry to FBI special agent. While every young boy dreams of working for the FBI or CIA, a case like this was not what I would have ever imagined. I had only one full year under my belt of ministry at Lifeline, and this was the first real exposure I had to human trafficking.

Adrenaline began pumping and all I knew was that somehow, someway, we had to rescue Betty. She begged us not to call the police. She said that she had called 911 months earlier, but that her captors drugged her to conceal her captivity. Instead of her freedom, she ended up with only a week of relief while she was held in lockup for drug use. Once freed, the sexual assault and abuse only intensified. She explained that the hotel "had eyes" and that no one could be trusted.

Betty was a brilliant young woman. After high school, she joined the military in order to go to college and pursue a career. Eventually, she retired from the military, came back to Alabama to work, and became involved with the wrong crowd. Despite the trauma of her captivity, Betty charted the patterns of her captors and gave us specifics on the times that she was usually alone. Additionally, she gave us the code name, "Red," that was used for the man in direct charge of her by the "customers."

Decidedly, we hatched the rescue operation. Betty told us that every night from around midnight until about 2 A.M. she was alone. To give her an opportunity to escape, we had local friends prepay for a 12:30 A.M. cab ride from the hotel to the Greyhound bus station. We also purchased a 1:15 A.M. bus ticket from her town to Birmingham, where Lord willing, she would arrive to us around 5:45 A.M. The plan was in place and the transportation paid. Now all that was left was to inform Betty of the plan.

I called the hotel and asked for room 107. The operator asked for the name of the guest, and I told him in the best shady voice I could muster, "I have money, and I need Red." Instantly, the call was transferred. My heart began to race only to hear the weary but familiar voice of Betty. Quickly, I told her to walk out of the hotel at 12:30 A.M. and that the cab we had paid for would be waiting with a sign in the window reading "Life." I told her that as soon as the cab arrived, we had instructed the driver to briefly and softly tap the horn. She whispered "Okay," and then I heard "Red." He was swearing and asking who was on the phone.

Thinking quickly and clearly, Betty told him that it was a prospective client and gave the phone to "Red." Again, I put on my best shady street voice impersonation, and I asked him for the cost and the available times. He hesitantly gave me the info, gave me a better number to call for future booking purposes, and then we hung up. I wanted to vomit.

Now all we could do was wait and pray. It's odd, but never once during this ordeal did we think that perhaps Betty was joking with us or using us. I believe it's in those moments that the Holy Spirit confirms action and gives an extra boost of adrenaline to accomplish what He sets before you.

I remember praying for sweet Betty and asking that the Lord would allow her the opportunity to escape without harm and without consequence. One of our social workers along with her husband agreed to go to the bus station in a questionable part of downtown Birmingham to receive Betty, if the Lord allowed her to escape. If indeed our plan was successful, they would call me and we would take her to eat, to the grocery store, and to obtain some new clothes.

The call came in at 6 A.M. Betty had arrived. She had simply walked out, stepped into the cab, and never looked back. No one was around nor saw Betty leave. The Lord protected her, and she escaped.

There she was, a broken woman without dignity, bruised, and scarred but filled with hope. The humility by which she received our care over the next two hours did nothing more than prove that this was a very broken woman who needed rescue. It was such an honor that the Lord allowed us to step into Betty's story.

Long story short, we were able to get Betty to safety through Lifeline's maternity care housing ministry — Lifeline Village. Betty gave birth to a healthy baby girl whom she placed for adoption with a Christian family. Betty secured a job and had her dignity restored, but more importantly Betty's life was changed from a victim to victor when she came to saving faith in our Lord Jesus Christ.

You see, beloved, our God does infinitely more than we could ever imagine when we step willingly into the brokenness of the world with the light and the love of the gospel of Jesus Christ. The truth is, we need to start taking many more of those steps.

Trafficking of Image Bearers

Human trafficking, especially sex trafficking is an enormous problem throughout the world. According to the popular "End It Movement" there are over 40 million image bearers of God currently trapped in human trafficking, and these men, women, boys, and girls are voiceless — many times invisible though they are all around us.

The insidious practices of human traffickers rely on the dark and take place in the the sleaziest of brothels. Trafficking is also camouflaged to take place under our noses at places like the Atlanta airport or even Walt Disney World. No matter where it is taking place, it is rampant, disgusting, and prevalent worldwide.

In 2015, *HuffPost* reported extensively on the prevalence of human trafficking happening at the Walt Disney World Resort in Florida. In an undercover sting, 11 Disney employees were arrested who had either aided or abetted these operations.

No matter where trafficking occurs, it originates from the pit of hell. Trafficking reduces image bearers to property which another image bearer consumes and then discards. We must take a bold stance against human trafficking.

The Fuel of Human Trafficking

While most could never imagine fueling or participating in human trafficking and prostitution, many evangelical Christians have allowed themselves to become willing consumers and users. As a matter of fact, the U.S. is the greatest generator for the demand for human trafficking. You might scratch your head and ask, "How?"

Pornography fuels human trafficking in the same way that kindling fuels a fire. Most of the pornographic industry relies heavily on prostitution, human trafficking, and sex trafficking. The consumption of pornographic materials demands a never-ending stream of "subjects" to satisfy an endless need for more gratification. The subjects of pornographic media come primarily from the poor, the needy, the orphan, and the trafficked.

Tim Challies, author and purveyor of Challies.com, reports many alarming statistics about the pornography industry. First, according to Challies, "In 2016, people watched 4.6 billion hours of pornography at just one website (the biggest porn site in the world). That's 524,000 years of porn or, if you will, around 17,000 complete lifetimes. In that same time people watched 92 billion videos (or an average of 12.5 for every person on earth)."

Katie Van Syckle, reporting for *The New York Times* in March 2018, is quoted as a porn industry expert. "As I started reporting on adult film, I approached it as a beat like any other and I found that performers wanted to talk," Van Syckle wrote. "They understood their significance in American culture, even if no one else did. Whatever you think about adult film, it is one of the most consumed forms of media in the world. Exact figures for the size of the industry are scarce, but experts put total sales around a billion dollars a year."

The article mentions that one pornographic Internet site alone draws 80 million visitors a day. She said, "Studies show that adult film has become merely a form of sex education for young people around the world."

Beloved, this isn't just a problem, this is an epidemic. Remember that these statistics come from a single website (albeit the largest online distributor of pornographic materials). According to Challies, so many people are using porn that it is indeed impossible to tabulate the complete usage.

What's even more frightening, Challies reports, is that 80% of pornography users feel absolutely no guilt for their use of pornographic materials. Challies says,

> We know that any sin, when repeated over time, begins to deaden the conscience. Those who at first felt guilt about pornography soon come to find their conscience hardened, then seared. Porn is so available, so common, so celebrated, and so widely-used, that many people have lost even that inner sense that it is wrong.

Lest you begin to think that the demand might curb in the next generation, the statistics indicate otherwise. Ninety-six percent of young adults state that they are either encouraging, accepting, or neutral in their view toward pornography — 17% talk about porn in a positive way; 43% accept it as if it's just a reality of life in this world; 36% don't consider it a moral issue at all.

We must also understand that this consumption is not sporadic, but routine. Forty-nine percent of young adults admit to using porn on a daily basis, while 57% of young adults and 46% of all men admit to seeking out porn at least once per month.

The reason for these lackadaisical responses to pornography among young adults include both the wide spread availability as well as early exposure to graphic content. Challies found that,

> ...at age 11, the average child has already been exposed to explicit pornographic content through the Internet. Ninety-three percent of boys and 62% of girls are exposed to Internet-based pornography during their adolescent years and 22% of the vast quantities of porn consumed by people aged under 18 is consumed by those aged less than 10.

To add to that, the vast number of these adolescents and consumers of pornography are accessing it on a mobile phone. In the U.S., 70% of all porn consumed is watched on a mobile phone, while the world wide mobile consumption is 61%.

As I have traveled the world in the last 16 years, the biggest change that I have seen the world over, is the advancement of personal technology. I have been in the bush in Uganda, where no one had running water, but almost every single person had a smartphone. We are a completely connected people which comes with immense blessings, but also abundant temptation and opportunity for the devil to wreak havoc.

Beloved, this is not just a battle for the *Imago Dei*, this is a battle for the hearts and souls of our sons and daughters. Parents, we cannot be negligent in protecting the eyes, hearts, and minds of our children.

Today, you can't even casually watch a college football game and not have your home barraged with the sensual soft porn from advertisers. So many advertisers have flocked to pornographic content to sell products such as burgers, Internet domains, cars, hygiene products, and so much more that we are becoming numb through overexposure. We must not only be vigilant to protect our children, but also to teach them why these images pose such a great risk and such a present danger.

Parents, we also must be dutiful to restrict access for as long as we can. Currently, I teach a ninth grade small group at our church. I have been with this group for the last three-plus years since they were in sixth grade. I was shocked as to how many of my sixth grade boys had Apple iPhones with unlimited data plans. Parents, it is nothing short of negligent if we fail to take steps to protect our children from being exposed to pornography.

If you want to take a stance today to protect image bearers who are being trafficked and used to fuel this scandalous industry, the first thing you can do is to protect the image bearers in your own home. For some practical steps to take to protect your children from pornography, see Challies' blog on protecting your home. I have found this post incredibly helpful — www.challies.com/articles/the-porn-free-family-plan.

Some specific things our family has found helpful to protect our children are:

- Limit technology from bedrooms,
- Install Disney Circle® on our Wi-Fi,
- Require that iPods® with internet be used only during free time and for limited amounts of time
- Openly talk about usage with our children, letting them know that anything they do on a device in our home is up for open scrutiny.

When it comes to pornography, it is not just Internet sites, magazines, and viewing images of strangers with which we must concern ourselves. Instead, we have to be concerned about exposure from those close to our children as well. Our culture has become so sexualized that the first pornography a child may come in contact with might be of a friend or teacher.

Challies says, "Young people are using their digital devices to trade in self-porn; there is immense pressure on young women to send photos of themselves to young men (who, of course, can never be trusted with such photos)." And it is rampant when 62% of teens and young adults state they have received a sexually explicit image, with 41% having sent the image to a boyfriend or girlfriend. Challies continues, "Women are more likely to both send and receive these nude images, presumably because it has become part of the dating ritual that women send nude or nearly-nude photos of themselves to boyfriends or potential boyfriends."

These statistics are proof of the truth which the Apostle Paul penned to the church at Rome in Romans 1:20-25:

> For His invisible attributes, namely, His eternal power and divine nature, have been clearly perceived, ever since the creation of the world, in the things that have been made. So they are without excuse. For although they knew God, they did not honor Him as God or give thanks to Him, but they became futile in their thinking, and their foolish hearts were darkened. Claiming to be wise, they became fools, and exchanged the glory of the immortal God for images resembling mortal man and birds and animals and creeping things. Therefore

God gave them up in the lusts of their hearts to impurity, to the dishonoring of their bodies among themselves, because they exchanged the truth about God for a lie and worshipped and served the creature rather than the Creator.

Oh beloved, it crushes my heart because we have truly traded the truth of God for a lie. This sex-crazed culture is looking for anything and everything to fill the vast void in their lives. Every single person has a deep longing in their lives placed there by God which can only be filled by Him. Nude images of a co-worker, boyfriend, or stranger will do nothing more than to further dig out the emptiness. It may temporarily give a rush or high, but it can't be sustained.

> *Every single person has a deep longing in their lives placed there by God which can only be filled by Him.*

The image bearers of God were destined for something so much more. I love what C.S. Lewis says in *Mere Christianity* about desire:

Creatures are not born with desires unless satisfaction for these desires exists. A baby feels hunger; well, there is such a thing as food. A duckling wants to swim; well, there is such a thing as water. Men feel sexual desire; well, there is such a thing as sex. If I find in myself a desire which no experience in this world can satisfy, the most probable explanation is that I was made for another world.

Lewis goes on to write more about desire in his famous work, *The Weight of Glory*:

It would seem that our Lord finds our desires not too strong, but too weak. We are half-hearted creatures, fooling about with drink and sex and ambition when infinite joy is offered us, like an ignorant child who wants to go on making mud pies in a slum because he cannot imagine what is meant by the offer of a holiday at the sea. We are far too easily pleased.

Our culture today is attempting to fill the grand desire of the sacred with the mud of the secular which will leave them nothing more than needy. The pornographic is stealing the heart, soul, and mind of our culture while simultaneously fueling human trafficking and slavery.

Looking at the numbers it is almost certain that many reading this are struggling with a pornography addiction or are in denial as to its effects. First, I want you to know that there is hope for healing and grace.

Jesus didn't come to redeem His image bearers because we had it all together, but He came while we were sinners and depraved. We were dead in our trespasses and sin. We were strangers and by nature objects of wrath. The bounty price on our head was steep and high, but Jesus paid the price to redeem us and release us from bondage.

Beloved, you can be forgiven completely with your life hidden with Christ. Unlike in the Old Testament where the people had to make atonement continually for their sins, Jesus Christ has come once and for all to redeem us. And this should supply great confidence and perseverance through the gospel of grace. We are forgiven, and it's all through His unmerited favor and grace.

You can be forgiven and freed from being a statistic of pornography. However, make sure once you have tasted and seen the precious grace of the Lord that you repent and seek help. Pornography is an addiction, and you will need help and daily accountability. You need someone who will walk with you, pray for you, ensure that the images will be wiped clean from your life, and will help you to once again see others not as objects but in the image of an almighty God.

The Vulnerable Cannot Seem to Escape

As I mentioned previously, according to The United Nations International Children's Education Fund (UNICEF), there are 153 million orphaned and vulnerable children in the world. These numbers include children who have lost one or both parents to death and are compounded by the children who have been abandoned to an institution, or the streets, or are living in foster care. The vast majority of these children will never be adopted, and the majority are unadoptable.

Every single day 5,760 more children become orphaned while every minute two orphans age out with no family to belong to and no place to call home. This begs the question, "What happens to all of these children who are aging out?"

According to statistics, the destiny of most orphans is to move from one form of vulnerability to another. UNICEF estimates that 15% of aging out orphans will be imprisoned or dead by the age of 18. And of the millions of orphans each year who are pushed into a world without hope, family or a future, 75% will be trafficked or ensnared by prostitution. Seemingly, the most vulnerable cannot escape vulnerability, and this is no less true in the U.S. In fact, the statistics for U.S. foster care are just as grim as worldwide statistics.

Currently, the U.S. has almost 500,000 children in the foster care system, and all are at extremely high risk for poor outcomes. According to survey results reported by the *Los Angeles Times*, 80% of the incarcerated in the U.S. have spent time in the U.S. foster care system, while 90% of all foster youth will spend time in court for crime, with 25% of foster youth being incarcerated within two years of leaving the system.

The poor outcomes are not limited to crime. Studies indicate that 40-50% of former foster youth become homeless within 18 months after leaving care. For those who are able to find jobs, 60% will earn an income below the poverty line with only about 3% attending college. For many former foster youth, the downward spiral continues. It is estimated that well over 60% of those who age out of the U.S. foster care system will be trafficked or willingly enter into prostitution.

This is why I believe the Bible consistently speaks of justice for the vulnerable. This is why I believe Jesus rebuked His disciples when Mary Magdalene, a former prostitute, anointed His head with an alabaster jar of perfume and showered His feet with her tears. Jesus had compassion and took notice of the vulnerable, because no matter their condition, they bore the marks of His Father. The Bible tells us we are to take notice because their physical condition mirrors our spiritual condition before Christ.

Perhaps there is no clearer example than the scene in John 8. The Pharisees and teachers of the law had caught a woman committing adultery and they "brought" her out. The text suggests they were doing this to trap Jesus and test Him. Essentially, they were looking into a sordid situation in order to condemn the sinner and try to condemn Jesus. So they brought her before Jesus and John 8:4-5 reports their words, *"Teacher, this woman has been caught in the act of adultery. Now in the Law, Moses commanded us to stone such women. So what do You say?"*

Jesus is confronted with two types of prostitution in John 8, spiritual and physical, and He addresses both the same, with kind and loving rebuke. Jesus doesn't reprimand the Pharisees who have prostituted themselves to the law above the grace of God. Instead, He asks them to throw stones if they are without sin. Then Jesus bends down and begins to draw in the sand but what exactly He wrote was not recorded. Many have postulated that He was writing the sins of those standing around Him, but I believe He was lowering Himself to the level of the woman who had been caught.

As I travel the world, I am consistently put eye-to-eye and face-to-face with the world's most vulnerable. I have been in slums among human slaves. I have been face-to-face with household servants. I have played and worked among street children, and I have visited orphans with debilitating disease and sickness. In every situation, the posture of the most vulnerable is consistent: bowed down low to the ground.

John 8:8 says, *"And once more He (Jesus) bent down and wrote on the ground."* Beloved, I have to believe that this woman, who was dragged out from another man's bedroom, is in a humiliated state. One is certainly led to believe that she is not standing, but hunched over in shame in the dirt. I truly believe that

Jesus bent down to identify with this woman, to enter her world, and to show her mercy.

In many Asian cultures in which I have visited, they operate as an honor and shame culture. The most vulnerable are always expected to take a posture lower than one with more honor or power. Beloved, this is not how we are to treat fellow men and women made in the image of our Creator. In these settings, the Lord has led me to get on the floor in front of household servants until I get them to lift their heads. Although I cannot speak their language, I want to give them dignity and purpose, because ultimately we are all level at the foot of the Cross. It is remarkable to see the change in the countenance of these precious image bearers when I have stooped down to them. Household servants who would normally try to appear invisible begin to show their true personality. Showing the dignity of the gospel to the least of these is the call of the Christ follower.

This biblical discourse ends with Jesus restoring this woman. She stands and then He stands as well and says, *"Woman, where are they? Has no one condemned you?"* (John 8:10). The woman then reports the obvious, that they have all gone away. Then Jesus looks her in the eye to show her dignity, mercy, and love. We have to believe that His words gave her life and restored her soul. *Jesus says, "Neither do I condemn you; go, and from now on sin no more."* (John 8:11)

Sin begets more sin and vulnerability begets more vulnerability. We must be fierce defenders of life in the way we reach out to the vulnerable, because only the gospel of Jesus Christ and the presence of God's family can help the vulnerable escape the cycle of abuse, hurt, and entrapment.

Invest in One, Don't Be Overwhelmed

All of these statistics can be overwhelming, heart-breaking, and discouraging. It could either lead us to have a savior complex in which we believe that only we can save them, or to become apathetic because the need is so vast.

I want instead to encourage you to invest where you are planted. If every Christ-follower the world over would invest fully in their families and in their broader communities, we would begin to see a huge difference.

Instead of being overwhelmed or trying to do everything, begin investing intentionally in what the Lord has in front of you. Remember that Jesus, although He was God, didn't touch, heal, and minister to every single person in His path.

In John 14:12 Jesus says, *"Truly, truly, I say to you, whoever believes in Me will also do the works that I do; and greater works than these will he do, because I am going to the Father."*

Jesus invested deeply in 12 ordinary men with a more intimate investment in three — Peter, James, and John. Jesus' ministry lasted for a mere three years and in that time He healed many who were lame, blind, dead, and hungry. While that healing was only temporary, it signified a greater spiritual healing that would last forever. The miracles of Jesus were to testify to a much greater spiritual reality, not to fix all brokenness and to right all of society's ills.

Jesus didn't touch every person on earth physically, but He still did everything He was appointed to do. In the high priestly prayer that Jesus prays shortly before His crucifixion found in John 17, Jesus says in verse 4, *"I glorified you (Father) on earth, having accomplished the work that You gave Me to do."*

Beloved, rest assured that the end of human trafficking, the sex trade, and pornography doesn't depend on you, but it can start with you. We must be found faithful to do exactly what the Lord has appointed us to do and to do it to the best of our ability for His glory alone. Don't be discouraged or become apathetic, but invest in the gospel right where you are.

Let me give you an example. I have a pastor friend who adopted his youngest daughter as an infant. My friend, let's call him "John," and his wife, "Jane," told me his daughter's story which is ultimately encapsulated in the story of her birth mom. John's daughter's birth mother is a woman addicted to drugs who is owned by a pimp in a small southern town. The pimp provided this woman with drugs in order to make her dependent on him and to minimize the risk of her escaping.

As this woman was being violated, sold, and swapped around as a used book, she became pregnant with John's daughter. By God's divine providence, she was discovered by a Christian lawyer in town. This attorney, let's call her "Marsha," bought this vulnerable pregnant woman from the pimp. Marsha loved on her, nurtured her, and encouraged her toward adoption. The woman chose to place her baby with my friends, John and Jane. John shared with me that their prayer was that their baby girl's birth mother would stay in relationship and that her life would be dramatically changed.

Sadly, in the end, this broken woman returned to the streets. John and Jane haven't seen her since the adoptive placement; however, I love the attitudes of John and his wife toward her. John said, "All we can do is pray for her daily, trusting the Lord to turn her heart, mind and life. In the meantime we will love, nurture, and train our daughter toward Christ." John knows he can't save every woman who has been trafficked, and he knows he can't change his daughter's birth mother's heart, but he can be found faithful to do what is in front of him.

In the meantime, the difficulty of this story isn't the end of the story either. Marsha has begun a ministry where she is rescuing pregnant women who are caught in prostitution through her law practice and doing everything she can to see gospel transformation in their lives while encouraging adoption for the babies.

We aren't called to do everything, but we can all do something.

Modern Day Slavery

According to the International Justice Mission (IJM) there are more human slaves and indentured servants today than at any other time in history.

While in the U.S. we may have believed that slavery ended after Lincoln's Emancipation Proclamation and the end of the Civil War, but that is a far cry from the truth.

Modern day slavery doesn't just include human and sex trafficking but also land theft, indentured servitude, police abuse of power, and forced labor of the poor. In many countries men and women are forced to sell themselves and their families into slavery in order to survive. We all acknowledge that it is wrong to believe that you own or control another person. There is one God and one Christ, and He is over all things. If we believe that our God is sovereign and in control, we must disaffirm any person's right to sovereignty over another in all circumstances. He appoints man his days and forms all life from the dust. It is utterly arrogant to lord yourself over another person.

The Caste System Denies the *Imago Dei*

In India, where the caste system is alive and well, there are more slaves than in any other country in the world. The caste system establishes and orders the worth of individuals. Those in the lowest castes have limited to no opportunity, and many are even seen as "untouchable" and valued less than street animals. Those in lower castes are forced to sell themselves and their families into backbreaking slavery in order to survive another day. In my many trips to India, I have seen buildings built on the backs of these indentured slaves. I have seen men and women whipped and beaten to the point of near brokenness.

It is beyond appalling to see one made in the image of God treat another with such brutality. While India's infrastructure is growing, do not be misguided — India is growing on the backs of modern day slaves. The story yet to be told is of the children of India who have been born into a lower caste and into slavery. We should not be surprised. The Scriptures warn of evildoers who seek to profit from the vulnerability of others, and there are plenty of slave owners in India that prey upon the hardship of low birth. This is but one example of the ravages of slavery.

According to IJM, countless people are sold into slavery every day even as slave owners profit to the tune of $1 billion off of their misery. IJM encourages believers the world over to unite to end slavery by rescuing slaves, bringing justice to slave owners, and working for laws which would irradicate the slave trade .

IJM, and other Indian indigenous groups, are working tirelessly to end human slavery while also rescuing and buying children out of slavery. One such ministry is a strategic partner of Lifeline's in India. STEPS Home in Chennai, India, is run by my brother Isaac Manogarom and his wife Tara. Their story is much too long to tell here, but in short, they have redeemed more than 18 young ladies out of slavery and given them a home. They disciple these young ladies, teach them life skills, and educate them with the best the country has to offer.

The Manogarom's own story is built upon the caste system. Tara was born into a Brahmin family, which is the highest, priestly caste. Isaac was born into a family of one of the lowest castes. Their extended families still detest their marriage greatly; however, because they are both precious believers in the Lord Jesus Christ, they knew that no caste system could define them. It saddens my heart to think of the way cultures the world over rank their people in a progression of significance. This is a direct affront to the Creator who made us all. Paul proclaims in Galatians 3:28, *"There is neither Jew nor Greek, there is neither slave nor free, there is no male and female, for you are all one in Christ Jesus."*

I love my time visiting STEPS and hearing the girls sing of their freedom in Christ. I tear up every time I see the joy in the eyes of these precious girls because I know they are now safe, loved, and well-nurtured. My heart breaks though for the millions of children just like these girls who are the youngest and most vulnerable victims of human slavery.

Beloved, we must love mercy, seek justice, and walk humbly with our God for the sake of seeing fellow image bearers of Christ freed from the bonds of physical and spiritual slavery because that is what it means to be pro-life.

Discussion Questions

1. Reflecting on Betty's story, is there anything holding you back from stepping into the brokenness of human trafficking? Be honest about any discomforts or fears.

2. What systems do you have in place to protect yourself and your kids from purposefully or accidentally encountering pornography? If nothing, what systems can you add?

3. How have you seen the truth of Romans 1:20-25 present in our world or in your own life or family?

4. Do you or someone you know need to be reminded of the atonement and forgiveness that came with Christ's sacrifice? If so, who can you help remind or who can remind you?

5. While we can't do everything, what is one thing you can do to aid the vulnerable?

Chapter Eleven

IDENTITY

With the onset of the theological negligence of neo-orthodoxy,
we have created a generation of "Christians" who blame the Holy Spirit
for their sinful desires ("God made me this way, and it's a proof of
good fruit when I act in accordance with my heart's desires").
Thus, from the epoch of late modernity onward, the gospel
is on a collision course with the idol of sexual freedom.

— Rosaria Butterfield in the foreword of Christopher Yuan's book,
Holy Sexuality and the Gospel

Conservative evangelical Christians in the U.S. may feel as though the nation's heart was lost on June 25, 2015, with the Supreme Court's decision in *Obergefell v. Hodges*. This landmark decision ushered in the legalization of same-sex marriage and added much ambiguity to the meaning of marriage in the U.S.

Evangelicals scurried quickly in the days after posturing a response and asking themselves the question, "How did we get here so quickly?" The problem is, we didn't get there at lightning speed. Instead, the journey to a redefinition of marriage was a slow fade away from the Word of God and a pro-life ethic. I think we can trace the beginning of this journey much further to September 4, 1969, when then-California governor and adoptive father, Ronald Reagan, signed into California law "The Family Law Act of 1969." This new law essentially allowed for anyone to seek a divorce without causation, thus coined "no-cause divorce."

The stated purpose of the law was to allow a spouse to seek a divorce without tarnishing the reputation of the other and/or without perjuring themselves in creating sufficient reason to legally divorce their spouse. What God had issued, "let no man tear apart," the State of California essentially reissued as, "let anyone break for any reason or no reason at all."

Every state in the union followed suit with no-fault divorce laws like dominoes falling in rapid succession. I don't believe we can overstate the importance of this decision, or the consequence of this law as it essentially ushered in a wave of "sexual freedom and expression." Men and women are now legally free to treat marriage as a suggestion as it has become easier to both enter into and to dissolve a marriage than to trade in a car.

The period that followed in the 1970s was marked by the "free love" movement and sexual revolution. This time period is often described in positive terms as a time of "great sexual liberation." This social revolution challenged outright both biblical and traditional behavior related to sexuality and relationships. Accoring to Ruth Engs in *The Journal of Health and Medicine Through History,* "Sexual liberation included increased acceptance of sex outside of traditional heterosexual, monogamous relationships (primarily marriage)...The normalization of contraception, public nudity, pornography, premarital sex, homosexuality, masturbation, alternative forms of sexuality, and the legalization of abortion all followed." Logic follows if marriage is no longer a sacred and legally binding union of a man and woman, then there is increased "freedom" to "love the one you're with."

Reproductive freedom was the buzzword of the 1970s and 1980s. If you are going to grant freedom to explore all of your sexual options, then you better have the "get out of jail free card" of contraception and abortion to limit the consequences. A created purpose of intimacy was to "be fruitful and multiply," but in a society that ignores the Creator, this command to bear children is perceived as burdensome, and the ability to procreate is nothing more than an inconvenient consequence of sexual freedom.

The fruit of the sexual revolution has influenced us all. We have forgotten how to blush. In the late 1980s and throughout the 1990s, the concept of family was completely realigned in movies and sitcoms, and we sat by laughing with ever limited discomfort. Main characters on our favorite shows lived together, slept around as a sport, and mocked the idea that marriage was sacred.

The hit TV sitcoms of the 1990s were *Seinfeld* and *Friends*, which still to date are among the top ten sitcoms in television history. These shows mixed a wisecracking style with a cesspool of crude sexuality and crass humor. The characters were trying on sexual partners like clothes in a dressing room, and their sexual behavior was praised and celebrated. Next, we introduced the normalization of same-sex attraction, identity, and relationship. Beginning with MTV's introduction of Pedro Zamora as the first openly gay cast member, we have seen an increasing presence of homosexual characters in mainstream entertainment. Beloved, this public redefining of sexual ethics didn't come out of nowhere. It came as a result of our apathy and our idolatry of sex, self, and entertainment.

> *It is He who made the earth by His power, who established the world by His wisdom, and by His understanding stretched out the heavens. When He utters His voice there is a tumult of waters in the heavens, and He makes the mist rise from the ends of the earth. He makes lightning for the rain, and He brings forth the wind from His store-houses. Every man is stupid and without knowledge; every goldsmith is put to shame by his idols, for his images are false, and there is no breath in them. They are worthless, a work of delusion; at the time of their punishment they shall perish. Not like these is He who is the portion of Jacob, for He is the one who formed all things, and Israel is the tribe of His inheritance; the Lord of hosts is His name.*
> —Jeremiah 51:15-19

Today's pervasive worldview disregards God in either atheistic denial or agnostic indifference. While in California recently, I noticed many stretches of road sponsored by "Atheist United" instead of your local Lions Club

International. We have completely denied that there is a God and that there is any order. This is all done in an effort to justify our behavior and idolatry, because where there is no God, there is no guilt or law. Without guilt and absolute truth, we no longer have to worry about our behavior being labeled as "wickedness," but we can conveniently name it "choice" or "the way I was born." Jeremiah prophesied about this over 2,500 years ago and warned that this thought would lead to great shame.

If we tacitly accept this worldview and thereby live lives that seemingly affirm that there is no God, then we endorse the notion that there is no Creator. If there is no Creator, then people are just a random part of the cosmos, not the crown of creation and certainly not an absolute design. This pervasive materialistic worldview leads to utter confusion in all matters of life including our understanding of gender and sexual identity.

Romans 1:25 is heard in the refrain of this worldview as it tells us that we have exchanged the glory of God for a lie and now worship our philosophies and our ability to choose the way we think creation should be ordered. *"They exchanged the truth about God for a lie and worshipped and served the creature rather than the Creator, who is blessed forever!"*

Al Mohler, President of The Southern Baptist Theological Seminary in Louisville, Kentucky, said, "To every image bearer we owe respect, but we do not owe an understanding that every single individual has a right to define who he or she is and demand that the world has to come to terms with it." When we determine that God-given gender, sexual orientation, and order is arbitrary and open to interpretation, it is a personal affront to the Creator, Author and Sustainer of the universe."

Imagine that I went to an exhibit on the work of impressionist artists at a renowned art gallery. Then once at the exhibit I began to assign arbitrary meaning and thought to the works of art and the artist's interpretation. I assign meaning to paintings that were never intended by the artist. If I articulate my opinions with confidence, I could be mocked as someone who doesn't understand art. I could be labeled as ignorant and uncultured. I might even be asked to leave because I don't have the right to determine what someone else's art means.

To take it a step further, if I wrote a book that Vincent van Gogh's *The Starry Night* was really about life on the sun, it would be censured and scorned. I could argue that van Gogh was highly troubled, depressed and a bit insane. While I would be right, I would still have no right to assign a meaning to the work of this great artist. The reasoning is simple; the creator or the artist has the right to define the meaning, the reason, and the significance of their art work.

Beloved, we are insulting the Creator and the God of this universe when we state that gender or sexual orientation is fluid and can be decided by each and every person. Gender and sexual orientation is something that the Bible affirms as a matter of God's revelation. Indeed, it's a matter of the creation that God has brought about to His glory. When He created human beings, the only beings in His image, He created us, male and female.

> Then God said, 'Let us make man in our image, after our likeness. And let them have dominion over the fish of the sea and over the birds of the heavens and over the livestock and over all the earth and over every creeping thing that creeps on the earth.' So God created man in his own image, in the image of God He created him; male and female He created them. —**Genesis 1:26-27**

> "This is the book of the generations of Adam. When God created man, He made him in the likeness of God. Male and female He created them, and He blessed them and named them man when they were created. —**Genesis 5:1-2**

Beloved, we were made in the image of God and assigned by gender and order, "in the beginning."

In his book, *Holy Sexuality and the Gospel*, Christopher Yuan writes,

> The world tells those of us with same-sex attractions that our sexuality is the core of who we are. God's Word paints quite a

different picture. Genesis 1:27 informs us that we are all created in the image of God. The Apostle Paul says that in Christ "we live and move and have our being (Acts 17:28)." Thus, my identity is not gay, ex-gay, or even straight. My true identity is in Jesus Christ alone.... In the conversation around sexuality, this subtle shift has created a radically distorted view of personhood.

Before we point fingers at all of those who define themselves as LGBTQ+, we cannot miss that the breakdown of the nuclear family is the primary wound that these precious image bearers carry in their hearts and souls. Husbands have stopped loving their wives like Christ loved the Church and instead rule over their families like a tyrant addicted to much sport and drink. Men are absent or harsh to their children and rarely, if ever, tell their children, "I love you."

In their book, The Blessing — Giving the Gift of Love and Unconditional Acceptance, Robert Trent and Gary Smalley share the following story:

"Please say that you love me, please!" Brian's words trailed off into tears as he leaned over the now still form of his father. It was late at night in a large metropolitan hospital. His tears revealed a deep inner pain and sensitivity that had tormented him for years, emotional wounds that now seemed beyond repair.

Brian had flown nearly halfway across the country to be at his father's side in one last attempt to try to reconcile years of misunderstanding and resentment. For years Brian had been searching for his father's acceptance and approval, but they always seemed just out of reach.

Brian's father had been a career Marine officer. His sole desire for Brian when he grew up was that he would follow in his father's footsteps. With that in mind, Brian's father took every opportunity to instill in his son discipline and the backbone he would need when one day he too was an officer. Words of love or tenderness were forbidden. It was almost as if any slip into a display of warmth might crack the tough exterior Brian's father was trying to create in his son.

Brian was driven by his father to participate in sports and to take elective classes that would best equip him to be an officer. Brian's only praise for scoring a touchdown or doing well in a class was a lecture on how he could and should have done even better.

After graduating from high school, Brian did enlist in the Marine Corps. It was the happiest day of his father's life. However, his joy was short-lived. Cited for attitude problems and a disrespect for orders, his son was soon on report. After weeks of such reports (which included getting into a vicious fight with his drill instructor), Brian was dishonorably discharged from the service as "incorrigible."

The news of Brian's dismissal from the Marines dealt a death blow to his relationship with his father. He was no longer welcome in his father's home, and for years there was no contact between them.

During those years, Brian struggled with feelings of inferiority and lacked self-confidence. Even though he was above average in intelligence, he worked at various jobs far below his abilities. Three times he had been engaged — only to break off the engagement just weeks before the wedding. Somehow he just didn't believe that another person could really love him.

We began counseling with Brian after he had broken his second engagement. As he peeled away the layers of his past, Brian began to see both his need for his family's blessing and his responsibility for dealing honestly with his parents. That is when the call came from his mother saying that his father was dying from a heart attack.

Brian went immediately to the hospital to see his father. The entire flight he was filled with hope that now, at long last, they could talk and reconcile their relationship. "I'm sure he'll listen to me. I've learned so much. I know things are going to change between us." Brian repeated these phrases over and over to himself during the flight, but it was not to be.

Brian's father slipped into a coma a few hours before he arrived. The words that Brian longed to hear for the first time — words of love and acceptance — now could never be spoken. Four hours after Brian arrived at the hospital, his father died without regaining consciousness.

"Dad, please wake up!" Brian's heartbreaking sobs echoed down the hospital corridor. His cries spoke of an incredible sense of loss; not only the physical loss of his father, but, like many others, also the emotional sense of losing any chance of his father's blessing.

Beloved, like Brian, we all were created in the image of God with an insatiable hunger to be loved by our creator. Fathers bear the earthly representation of what is a heavenly reality—the everlasting love of the Father. I truly believe that when dads became absent, divorce became easy, procreation became an inconvenience, and the marriage bed became permanently defiled, that identity was completely lost.

Sin is the pervasive pollutant to our true identity. It's how we are but not who we were meant to be. The desires of our hearts are corrupted just like Jesus said in Mark 7:21-22,

> *For from within, out of the heart of man, come evil thoughts, sexual immorality, theft, murder, adultery, coveting, wickedness, deceit, sensuality, envy, slander, pride, foolishness. All these evil things come from within, and they defile a person.*

Sin has polluted our identity and that loss of the identity of the *Imago Dei* has been incubated by the brokenness of families.

Truth in Love

It's neither politically correct nor expedient to identify the LGBTQ+ lifestyle as sinful, but it is, just as so many other lifestyles are, no matter their "orientation."

Yuan continues in his book,

> While guilt is a legal status of culpability, original sin is a moral condition. It means that our nature has been corrupted by sin, a condition that produces only more sin. This corruption is pervasive, impacting the entire human race. "None is righteous, no, not one" (Romans 3:10). This corruption is also pervasive in affecting the entire person. For each of us, sin affects all our faculties: actions, words, thoughts, and desires — including our sexual desires.

In the U.S., Christendom is divided on how to approach many who are a part of the LGBTQ+ lifestyle. The divide is so stark, and yet I believe also very unbiblical.

Many liberal mainline denominations and churches have chosen a posture of "love" over judgment. These churches accept LGBTQ+ as members and have whitewashed the sinful desire as a preconceived wiring that cannot be overcome. Love has really just become a pseudonym to these churches for complete and total acceptance.

On the contrary, many conservative churches have labeled anyone with even an inclination toward same-sex attraction as sinners who will be caught in the hands of an angry God. They rank the LGBTQ+ lifestyle as a unique abomination. It's as if they think that when Paul was listing the perversion of sins in Romans 1, he highlighted the parchment with neon markers, wrote with a Sharpie, and circled verse 27: "and the men likewise gave up natural relations with women and were consumed with passion for one another, men committing shameless acts with men and receiving in themselves the due penalty for their error."

It's shocking to see the intense castigation of same sex attraction against the relatively lesser reaction to blatant sins. It's as if the sins listed in verses 29-31 are mere suggestions of righteousness, worthy of less condemnation than an inclination toward sin. Both of these responses are harsh, unloving, and unbiblical. Jesus says, "You will know the truth, and the truth will set you free," in John 8:32. And then Matthew's gospel reports to us, *"When (Jesus) saw the crowds, He had compassion for them, because they were harassed and helpless, like sheep without a shepherd"* (9:36).

Then Paul sums it all up to the church at Ephesus in Ephesians 4:15-16,

> *Rather, speaking the truth in love, we are to grow up in every way into Him who is the head, into Christ, from whom the whole body, joined and held together by every joint with which it is equipped, when each part is working properly, makes the body grow so that it builds itself up in love.*

Tim Keller, founding pastor of Redeemer Presbyterian Church in New York City, said in a sermon, "Truth without love is imperious self-righteousness. Love without truth is cowardly self-indulgence. Both are selfish." John Newton, author of "Amazing Grace," once said, "Our natural temptation is to say what we should not say, or to not say what we should say. One is cruel arrogance, the other cruel cowardice, and neither is love." Friends, we should seek to speak the truth of Jesus Christ in love to one another. Such balance requires nothing less than the power and wisdom of Jesus Christ.

To illustrate the balance, a rebuke of a parent to a child is taken much better than that same rebuke from a stranger. Proverbs 27:4-7 says,

> *Wrath is cruel, anger is overwhelming, but who can stand before jealousy? Better is open rebuke than hidden love. Faithful are the wounds of a friend; profuse are the kisses of an enemy. One who is full loathes honey, but to one who is hungry everything bitter is sweet.*

If we speak truth without love it is cruel, overwhelming and leads receivers' ears dull to the message. However, if we never speak truth and call our blind acceptance of any behavior "loving," we are deceiving ourselves. This is not love; this is indifference, apathy, and closer to hate than love. If my child is running into a busy road, I cannot just turn a blind eye because I do not want to hurt their feelings and interrupt their "pleasure." I cannot just merely hope that they will see how accepting I am, come to their senses, and flee their desire to enter into a busy roadway. Instead, when my child is about to step in front of a car and their pending peril, I yell the only truth I know, "Stop!" And then and only then do I run toward my child, scoop them up in my arms and say, "Daddy loves you so much but you could get really hurt." This behavior is both abundantly truthful and loving.

Same-sex attraction and gender dysphoria is sinful in the same way that the lust of a man for a woman is sinful. You can be born with both, just like we are born and bent toward anger and pride; however, we can't allow image bearers to take these desires into the busy street of action without yelling, "Stop." And then and only then, we must scoop them up in our arms and tell them we love them and do not want them to get eternally hurt.

Gender Has Meaning

In Genesis 1 after each day of creation, *"God saw that it was good."* Then in Genesis 2, when we get more play-by-play and detail into the creation of man, we see in verse 18 that God says, *"It is not good that the man should be alone; I will make him a helper fit for him."* Man is incomplete without woman

So the Lord takes a rib from Adam's side and fashions a *"helper"* that would be suitable for him and that could complete the image of God in man. Once man beholds woman, he says in Genesis 2:23, *"This at last is bone of my bones and flesh of my flesh; she shall be called woman, because she was taken out of man."*

And this is what God called good in Genesis 1:27 — that God had created man, male and female, in His image. It wasn't until after God had made two completely complementary genders that He was able to look at all creation and as in Genesis 1:31 see *"everything that He had made"* and see that *"it was very good."*

This is why it isn't good to have a male-dominated, male-centric or male-superior society because such culture is oppressive, unkind, and stoic. In the same, the current culture in America is female-dominant where the ideals are the feminine virtues. Such a society lacks what God designed to be the dominant attributes of godly males and alters it with the ideal that nurture and acceptance are better than order and absolutes.

For this reason, children seek out mom or dad to meet different needs uniquely. When my children were younger and would fall and scrape themselves, they were prone to seek out Ashley who was quick to scoop them up, show affection, and then care for their wounds. As my children have gotten older and have needs for security and safety, they tend to seek me out. Moms and dads meet their children's needs differently, and children were designed to need the unique nurture of parents of both genders. This certainly isn't saying that a dad can't be nurturing or that a mom can't provide protection; however, it does support that there is no such thing as gender superiority or gender fluidity.

In today's culture a lie is being broadcast that gender is a social construct and large numbers of people are accepting this distortion. Academia has adopted the idea so completely that now at most major colleges and universities, incoming students are asked to provide their preferred pronouns, such as he/she, him/her, his/hers, or gender non-specific like xi.

A column was recently published in *The New York Times* by Farhad Manjoo titled, "The Perfect Pronoun, Singular 'They.'" The columnist wrote,

> *I am your stereotypical cisgender, middle-aged suburban dad. I dabble in woodworking, I take out the garbage, and I covet my neighbor's Porsche. My tepid masculinity apparently rings loudly enough that most people call me, 'he' and 'him.' And that's fine; I will not be offended if you refer to me by those traditional uselessly gendered pronouns, but 'he,' is not what you should call me. If we lived in a just, rational, inclusive universe, one in which we were not also irredeemably obsessed by gender, there would be no requirement for you to have to guess my gender just to refer to me in the common tongue.*

Manjoo has written for many different periodicals and newspapers about gender issues, and he has some fairly radical but accepted opinions including a suggestion that all men should wear makeup. But in *The New York Times*, he called for the elimination of all gendered pronouns in favor of the word "they," used in the singular. Manjoo continued,

> So, if you write about me, tweet about me, or, if you're a Fox News producer working on a rant about my extreme politics, I would prefer if you left my gender out of it....Call me 'they,' as in, "Did you read Farhad's latest column? They've really gone off the deep end." And unless you feel strongly about your specific pronouns, which I respect, I would hope to call you "they" too, because the world would be slightly better off if we abandoned unnecessary gender signifiers as a matter of routine communication. Be a "him" or "her" or whatever else in the sheets, but consider also being a 'they' and a 'them' in the streets.

As a society we have lost the reality of the *Imago Dei*. We were created specially and specifically by the Author, Creator, and Sustainer of the universe. We have no right to consider him wrong and say that the plumbing and DNA of a person are of no consequence. Honestly, this idea is as silly as it is devious.

A friend of mine who is a financial planner recently told me he was helping one of his particularly wealthy clients. This client is a celebrity known the world over, but to protect both my friend and his client, let's call the celebrity "Brian Smith" and my friend, "Peter."

Brian was meeting one afternoon with Peter to discuss his investments. Brian began telling Peter that he thought Christians were too narrow minded and closed to the LGBTQ+ agenda. Peter inquired why he thought this was so, to which Brian explained, "People should have the right to be whoever they want to be. We have no right to tell someone they can't be a man or woman, gay or straight, or whatever in the world they want to be."

Peter laughed and announced to his client, "I'm not sure we have met," to which Brian challenged, "Do what?!?" Then Peter continued, "Yes, my name is Brian Smith. I'm sure you must recognize me, I am very famous and extremely wealthy. Now that I've introduced myself, I need to go withdraw about $5 million dollars from one of my investments. Have a good day."

Brian, completely baffled declared, "Man, that's not funny." Then Peter looked right back at Brian and remarked, "You're right. It's not funny - just like it's not funny that we call truth a lie, or would tell someone they can be anyone whom they want to be."

Beloved, it's not funny. In fact, it's extremely sad, and it should break our hearts when image bearers war against the way that they were created. It should grieve our hearts when people exchange the truth about God for a lie. These lies are a slippery slope, and when we just accept them and move on, eventually humanity will suffer and crumble.

Mohler says,

> Christians have to speak sanity even if no one else does. It's because our understanding of humanity and of identity begins with God, begins with a Creator who made us for His glory, who determined not only where and when we would be born, but that we would exist, putting us on this earth and giving us an identity as His gift. Of course, there is some extent to which every single individual develops a self and develops personality, but that is fundamentally different from understanding that we determine our own identity.

The Slippery Slope

During the 2020 presidential election campaign, the Democratic Party has put forth over 20 candidates all vying for their party's nomination to run against the incumbent President Donald Trump. One particular candidate sparked mass interest for many reasons including: his youth, position as a mayor of South Bend, Indiana, and predominately because of his same-sex marriage.

Initially, Pete Buttigieg was praised and laureled as the first openly gay and same-sex married presidential candidate, but then in quick order he was passed over by the LGBTQ+ movement because they believed he wasn't "LGBTQ+" enough.

A June 18, 2019, opinion piece in *The New York Times* by Frank Bruni titled, "Pete and Chasten Buttigieg are a Traditional Wonder" stated,

> *Pete and Chasten Buttigieg celebrated their first wedding anniversary on Sunday. You know this if you're among Pete's roughly 1.1 million Twitter followers or Chasten's 340,000, because they traded sweetly effusive missives, as they frequently do. I've found myself wondering, what if Chasten were a 29-year-old straight woman instead of a 29-year-old gay man? What would that say about gender and double standards?*

Bruni goes on to conclude that Pete and Chasten are not gay enough nor do they really represent the LGBTQ+ lifestyle because they have adopted "traditional heterosexual gender roles." He makes the point that Chasten Buttigieg, a man, stays home and largely takes care of domestic concerns and took Mayor Pete Buttigieg's last name in formal context. Bruni calls this "a retro model of heterosexual marriage."

Bruni, who is openly gay and an outspoken advocate of LGBTQ+ issues, writes that he believes a woman cannot be fulfilled if she is simply at home taking care of "domestic issues," and primarily caring for the needs of the family. Bruni states,

> *That doesn't meet the new Democratic orthodoxy. If that doesn't meet the new Democratic orthodoxy for heterosexuals, how exactly does it function that the new orthodoxy is now reflected in the first openly gay homosexual couple to be celebrated as having a real possibility of residing in the White House?*

This is a slippery slope. What would have been unthought of even 12 years ago when Barack Obama, the first black president was making his run to the White House, is now described as antiquated. When you begin to tinker, alter, and subtly destroy the fabric of the family and gender which God so perfectly and intricately created, then you begin to decay an already sin-sick society.

Bruni concludes his article,

> I look at Chasten who, with Pete, landed on the cover of Time Magazine, and see at once how far gay people have come and how far women still have to go. I see what an imperfect patchwork progress is. To my previous thought experiments, add these: Would he and Pete get the same reception if they were men of color, or for that matter, didn't look so much like they just stepped out of a J. Crew catalog? What if they were a lesbian couple? Well, to each his own. Let people be true to themselves, no matter how daring, no matter how quaint.

Mohler has stated,

> Our ultimate meaning is never something that means we are true to ourselves. That might meet Shakespeare; it doesn't meet a biblical worldview. Being true to ourselves is not an adequate guide. We have to be true to what God has revealed. We have to be true to what God has intended. We have to be true to a reality that is indicated by Eden, not by a fallen world.

Beloved, we are truly living in a time where identity is marked by self-expression, not by God-ordained order and design. We are living in a time where parents continue to tell their children, "You can be anything you want to be," not simply referring to vocation but referring to gender as well.

To be truly pro-life doesn't mean we are homophobic or cruel and condemning. Instead we must be salt and light. We must love our LGBTQ+ neighbors as Christ loves them. We must invest heavily and lean in intentionally. We must never discard LGBTQ+ individuals in hate or condemnation, but hold them close with mercy and affection.

And once we have held them close and shown them our genuine love and affection, we must speak biblical truth. We must plead with them to repent and follow Christ. It isn't truly love or a pro-life ethic to never speak truth, in the same way that it isn't truthful or a pro-life ethic to be unloving. Speak the truth in love and love with the truth.

Parenting with an LGBTQ+ Landmine

Rosaria Butterfield and Christopher Yuan have both written books about coming out of lesbian and gay relationships, respectfully. They both left behind acting on their same-sex desire, repented, and followed Christ. While their testimonies of coming to Christ were different, their similarity is found in that both had believers who sought them out with love and truth, not condemnation, lies, or scorn.

Yuan wrote,

> You may ask, "How can I help someone with same-sex attractions when I don't personally struggle with it?" Then answer this: Since when do we have to struggle with a specific sin before we can help another with that same sin? Homosexuality isn't a psychological disorder or a developmental problem. To think that way is a futile, human-centered attempt to erase the reality of original sin. Let's call sin what it is. It's no surprise that the secular world tries to sanitize and erase sin. But when Christians view a homosexual orientation as neutral and innocent — simply an unchosen and persistent phenomenological pattern of same-sex attractions — could we be turning a blind eye to the doctrine of sin? If same-sex sexual attractions were only a natural consequence of the Fall, then they would be neutral — and, as some assert, potentially sanctifiable. However, if acting on same-sex attractions is sin, then there's nothing neutral or sanctifiable about it. Without doubt, same-sex relationships are sinful. But does this mean that heterosexuality — in all its forms — is blessed by God?

Yuan continues his reasoning that we are all born with a bent and desire for things which are sinful and ungodly. Who is righteous? Not a single one of us. And who has ever been born without any sinful sexual desire? The answer according to Paul in Romans 1 is the same, not a single one of us.

I was personally born with the desire to lust. When I found my precious wife Ashley and knew without a shadow of doubt that she would be my wife, I was filled with all manner of sexual desire for her. Every time I heard her say my name it was as if the Song of Solomon soundtrack was playing in my head.

By God's sweet and abundant grace I made it through high school and college and remained sexually pure, a virgin. However, the desire for my soon to be wife was so intense and so real that it cannot be denied, I was ready to consummate the wedding before we said the vows. Again, because of the grace of Jesus, a godly fiancé who at times was more spiritually mature than me, and the accountability of a dear friend, I didn't lose my virginity nor steal Ashley's from her until we said, "I do," before God and many witnesses.

Make no mistake, desire is real and that includes the desire for same-sex relationships and all matter of desire along the LGBTQ+ spectrum. The desire is temptation and not sin. The desire becomes sin when it masters us. This is why James says in James 1:14-18,

> But each person is tempted when he is lured and enticed by his own desire. Then desire, when it has conceived, gives birth to sin, and sin when it is fully grown brings forth death. Do not be deceived, my beloved brothers. Every good gift and every perfect gift is from above, coming down from the Father of lights, with whom there is no variation or shadow due to change. Of His own will He brought us forth by the word of truth, that we should be a kind of first fruits of His creatures.

Desire which is not mastered by the Holy Spirit leads to sin and death, but don't miss the good news. God gives the perfect gift of His Son and His grace which can conquer our selfish desires and purify us from sin. Let's be clear, same-sex attraction is real and many can be born with that predisposition; however, in the same way that the desire to commit adultery and fornication is real, if any are acted upon and not conquered by Christ, they lead to sin and death.

> The sting of death is sin, and the power of sin is the law. But thanks be to God, who gives us the victory through our Lord Jesus Christ.
> —1 Corinthians 15:56-57

All of those trapped in the LGBTQ+ lifestyle are not beyond the sweet grace of the Lord Jesus, but they must repent, lay their desire at the cross, and follow Him.

In 2 Corinthians 6:1-2, Paul says,

> Working together with Him, then, we appeal to you not to receive the grace of God in vain. For He says, "In a favorable time I listened to you, and in a day of salvation I have helped you." Behold, now is the favorable time; behold, now is the day of salvation.

Oh there is great hope for His grace. Let this passage harken us to the mission to preach the good news of the Kingdom of God to those who are perishing. We live in that time of great grace and patience. God is withholding His judgment and offering such sweet mercy for our rebellious hearts.

Remember that this day of salvation will not last forever but will only last for the time the Father has appointed. When the day of salvation is over, then the day of vengeance will arrive. There is an urgency to preach the gospel and proclaim the Kingdom to those who are perishing. There is urgency in our mission to manifest the pro-life gospel of the Kingdom to those with an identity crisis.

Therefore, parents, we must preach the gospel daily to our children. We must be consistent and biblical in our teaching. It is necessary that we teach our children the entire counsel of God and to live consistently with what we teach and believe.

Moms and dads, you will mess up and you will fail, that's as sure as the sun will set, so you must be quick to show your children your repentance, and must ask not only the Lord for forgiveness, but also ask your children for forgiveness for your hypocrisy. As parents, our children need our authenticity and our presence. Boys and girls created in the image of God do not need perfect earthly parents, but they need the imperfect parents they were assigned by God who are faithfully and genuinely living the faith on a daily basis.

Knowing that every image bearer will at some point be enticed by sinful and perverse sexual desire, we must talk early and often with our children about sex. This will make us uncomfortable and embarrassed, but it is a necessary step of discipleship. Now I am not saying this will be one of the easiest conversations to have with your kids; however, it is by far one of the most vital.

Ashley and I were personally mentored by dear friends Rob and Shawn Grubb who have also written material that I cannot recommend highly enough (developingsexualpurity@gmail.com). They counseled us to speak early and often about sex with our elementary aged children in age appropriate ways. By the time our children were in the fourth grade, the Grubbs highly recommended that we tell our children about a sexual union between a man and a woman. They told us to talk about the gift, the beauty, and the intimacy of sex the way that God created it. One of our goals of the conversation was to help our children see that sex is not a four-letter dirty word, but a gift, and one that we could openly talk about with them.

Only when they understood that God ordained sex and that we weren't the "experts," we could begin to tell them about how any gift of God can be sinfully distorted. We used the image of a fire in a fireplace. In the rightful place, a fire is beautiful, useful, and a desire to the eyes and body. However, a fire in your house which is outside of the fireplace and out of control will destroy you. Furthermore, even when the fire is in the fireplace, it must be tended to and guarded.

Friend, one way to guarantee that your children have a biblical view of sexuality is for you to have the tough conversations with them even when you are uncomfortable. If you don't educate your children on sex and sexuality, then someone else will. Most likely it will be a TV commercial, an ad for beer, an Internet porn site, their health textbook, a friend, and ultimately the sin-sick world.

The best way to guard the identity, heart, and sexual integrity of your child is to begin today daily preaching the gospel and discipling your children making sure they know that there is absolutely no topic off limits to discuss with you.

Lastly, when they ask you a question that you don't know how to answer, go to the Bible, prayer, or a trusted follower of Christ to make sure you provide a gospel-saturated response.

In today's world, we must acknowledge the topics of gender and sexuality are confusing and highly charged, and none of us feel completely competent to address them. Remember, we have a God who works through our frailty and limitation to put Himself on display. Be confident in Him and His ways, and he will lead you into Truth.

Discussion Questions

1. How have you witnessed the church abiding by Ephesians 4:15-16 when discussing sexuality and how have you witnessed the church abandoning it?

2. Are you tempted to believe the sins listed in Romans 1:39-31 are worthy of less condemnation than the sin listed in verse 27? How can that viewpoint be a stumbling block to your understanding of sin and to unbelievers you encounter?

3. How can you share the truth of scripture to those who believe gender is a social construct?

4. Discuss 1 Corinthians 15:56-57. How do you recognize both the crippling power of your sin and the even more powerful victory of our Savior?

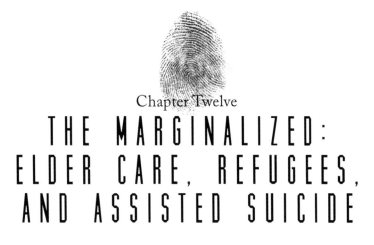

Chapter Twelve

THE MARGINALIZED: ELDER CARE, REFUGEES, AND ASSISTED SUICIDE

Come to me, all who labor and are heavy laden, and I will give you rest.

— Matthew 11:28

When Jesus, the long-awaited Messiah, first consummated His earthly ministry, He went to the place where the Jews would have expected — the synagogue. So it wasn't the location of His first act of public ministry that confounded the Jewish people, it was the opening message. Jesus goes to the synagogue in His hometown of Nazareth and reads from the scroll of Isaiah from what we now know as Isaiah 61.

> *And the scroll of the prophet Isaiah was given to Him. He unrolled the scroll and found the place where it was written, "The Spirit of the Lord is upon Me, because He has anointed Me to proclaim good news to the poor. He has sent Me to proclaim liberty to the captives and recovering of sight to the blind, to set at liberty those who are oppressed, to proclaim the year of the Lord's favor." And He rolled up the scroll and gave it back to the attendant and sat down. And the eyes of all in the synagogue were fixed on Him. And He began to say to them, "Today this Scripture has been fulfilled in your hearing."* —Luke 4:17-21*

Not what this hometown synagogue crowd expected. The familiar crowd first marveled at His words, but ultimately, they sought to destroy Jesus by throwing Him off a cliff. They wanted a Messainic superhero, not a suffering servant. They truly wanted a Messiah whose slogan was "Make Israel Great Again." However, Jesus came to proclaim justice and liberty to those who were captive. Jesus came to reclaim the *Imago Dei* and to redeem Creation from the curse of sin and death. As Sally Lloyd-Jones says in her award winning *Jesus Storybook Bible,* "Jesus came to make everything in the world right again. ... Jesus helped and healed many people. He made blind people see. He made deaf people hear. He made lame people walk. Jesus was making the sad things come untrue. He was mending God's broken world."

As pro-life image bearers of God, we are called to reach out to the marginalized, the elderly, the refugee, the oppressed, the weak, and all of those whom society labels as "less than." Indeed, we do this to mirror the life of our Savior, to show the gospel, and to help do our part in repairing creation.

Elder Care

Do not rebuke an older man but encourage him as you would a father, younger men as brothers, older women as mothers, younger women as sisters in all purity. —**1 Timothy 5:1-2**

You shall stand up before the gray head and honor the face of an old man, and you shall fear your God: I am the Lord. —**Leviticus 19:32**

Every decision has consequences, and every decision we make in contradiction to God's order and biblical revelation brings not only immediate consequences, but also many unintended future ramifications. In 1973, when the majority of nine U.S. Supreme Court justices decided to legalize abortion, they had no way of understanding the long-range social ramifications of this single decision any more than a different nine justices could potentially imagine the long-lasting affect of the 2015 decision to legalize same-sex marriage.

Because families are the backbone and basis of any healthy and thriving society, when we completely lose a pro-life ethic, families crumble. In 2019, The *Financial Times of London* published an article by Camilla Cavendish with the headline, "The Only Child is Becoming the Norm." She reports,

> *As populations shrink, we will have to redefine our notion of the family. The good news for the planet is that globally, families are shrinking. In 1964, the average woman had just over five children. By 2015, she had only 2.5. There are now 83 countries home to nearly half the world's population with fertility rates below replacement rates, roughly 2.1 births per woman.*

While the reporter celebrated this precipitous decline in the birth, fertility, and replacement rates, this is actually an imminent disaster. Cavendish makes it clear in her reporting that the environment and environmentalism are of much greater value to her than the command of the Bible to "be fruitful and multiply." This thought has its roots in the 1960s when warnings about a population explosion, mass starvation, and earthly destruction became the popular talking points. While mass starvation has yet to occur even as the population of the world expands, the radicalism of population control has had its effect on the 21st century, and the falling birth rate is a far greater threat to humanity than the feared expanding birth rate.

Cavendish goes on to write,

> *On Thursday, the Office for National Statistics announced that the birth rate in England and Wales in 2018 fell to 11.1 live births per 1,000 members of the population, the lowest rate since records began in 1938. Italy, once the home of romance and big Catholic families has hit the lowest birth rate this century, accentuated by record immigration. Japan's population shrank last year with a total fertility rate of 1.42. In the latter two countries, women are throwing off the shackles of family duties. One Japanese told me, "I wouldn't mind having a child, but I can't imagine putting up with a husband."*

One of the greatest gifts that the Lord bestowed to His image bearers was the gift of family. One of the imprints of God's design was the desire for communion. God answered this desire through the family. It was through the family that humanity would grow and flourish. The Lord has used the idea of family all throughout His Word to show His grace, His kindness, and His salvation. He told Abraham that He would make him into a great nation and that if he could number the stars, then he would be able to count the number of his "descendants" or family members.

Similarly, the Lord uses the beautiful imagery of adoption in the New Testament in Romans 8, Ephesians 1, and Galatians 3 and 4 to show that He is creating a multi-ethnic family who would care and provide for one another. Consequently, in Acts 2 and 4 when believers come to faith in Christ and are indwelt with the Holy Spirit, they immediately begin providing for the needs of others.

> Now the full number of those who believed were of one heart and soul, and no one said that any of the things that belonged to him was his own, but they had everything in common. And with great power the apostles were giving their testimony to the resurrection of the Lord Jesus, and great grace was upon them all. There was not a needy person among them, for as many as were owners of lands or houses sold them and brought the proceeds of what was sold and laid it at the apostles' feet, and it was distributed to each as any had need.
> —Acts 4:32-35

And now Cavendish and others describe the family as a prison or shackles. She continues to write,

> Only children are becoming the norm. In the United Kingdom, 40% of married couples have only one child. And among unmarried cohabiting couples and single parents, the share is even higher. A shrinking world will challenge us to redefine our notion of family, and to build different support networks for old age. But it should also be positive for the planet if we can tackle the continuing population growth in Africa.

She is right if in only one thing; fewer children is going to mean that there will be fewer family bonds and that, ultimately, it's not only children who will suffer, but the elderly and aged as well.

I am an only child, but not for the reasons mentioned in this article. For many and varied reasons, I was the only child born to my parents. Growing up, this reality did bring some distinct advantages. I always had the attention of my parents when it was needed, and I was able to travel the world with them because the expense of one tag-on was certainly far less than multiple.

For whatever benefits I might be able to articulate, I also know there will be challenges as my parents age, and one of those is the care of my parents. It is abundantly clear that the Lord has appointed me to care for my parents, especially as we approach the time when our roles will reverse and I assume the role of protector, defender, and provider.

I have seen my own father, my mother-in-law, and my dear friend Dr. Rick Morton walk through the journey of being an only child caring for aging parents. It is all of our God-given responsibility and duty to show grace and hospitality to our parents, but as an only child, I realized I am alone in this endeavor because I have no siblings to help.

I watched my dad care for his parents, especially my widowed grandmother. Although he loved every minute of her life, I watched him work, make decisions, and grieve alone without the comradery of siblings or extended family. Similarly, I watched my mother-in-law, a single mother of six, tirelessly care for her mom and then her widower father. She traveled back and forth between Georgia and North Carolina making sure both her children and her dad were shown gracious love and support. While I'm confident my mother-in-law would not have changed a thing about her involvement, I cringed when I realized all of the responsibility was squarely on her shoulders.

I understand that one day, the strength of my own parents will fail and that I alone am there to care for them. The problem is today in our culture many children feel as though their parents are merely a burden. As a whole, we live in a society that dismisses the aged and elderly as the "walking dead" with little to no value.

Beloved, you can't call yourself pro-life if you aren't willing to care for your aging parents or you breeze past a slow-moving older woman as if she is a speed bump. These beautifully aged and most mature among us are made in the image of God, and while their physical selves may be fading away because of the effects of a fallen world, they are due dignity, respect, concern, and defense.

Think about the amount of wisdom that is bound up in the retirement home or nursing facility closest to you. There are men and women who have learned life's hardest lessons either through success or failure. There are image bearers who still have so much to offer in wisdom and experience where motor skills are lacking.

Throughout the Bible, the widow is inextricably connected to the orphan and the vulnerable. As God's people, we are called to care for the elderly and the widow. The psalmist begs in Psalm 71:9, *"Do not cast me off in the time of old age; forsake me not when my strength is spent."* Unfortunately, the elderly need to have this prayer on their tongues and in their hearts continually in this generation, because unnatural death is creeping at their door. As a society and world we are advocating more for euthanasia and physician-assisted suicide than we are for abortion.

The Lord tells His people in Isaiah 46:4: *"Even to your old age I am He, and to gray hairs I will carry you. I have made, and I will bear; I will carry and will save."* If we do not care for the elderly and the terminally ill, then we have replaced the sovereignty of God's rule and reign with the idols of self and convenience.

Euthanasia and Suicide

And he said, "Naked I came from my mother's womb, and naked shall I return. The Lord gave, and the Lord has taken away; blessed be the name of the Lord." —Job 1:21

When a doctor graduates from medical school, it is common to swear to an oath. The historic practice for this commitment began in 5 B.C. with the invention of medicine and healing arts named after the first Greek "doctor," Hippocrates.

Translated into English, the oath states:

> I will apply dietetic measures for the benefit of the sick according to my ability and judgment; I will keep them from harm and injustice.

> I will neither give a deadly drug to anybody who asked for it, nor will I make a suggestion to this effect. Similarly I will not give to a woman an abortive remedy. In purity and holiness I will guard my life and my art.

> I will not use the knife, not even on sufferers from stone, but will withdraw in favor of such men as are engaged in this work.

> Whatever houses I may visit, I will come for the benefit of the sick, remaining free of all intentional injustice, of all mischief and in particular of sexual relations with both female and male persons, be they free or slaves.

> What I may see or hear in the course of the treatment or even outside of the treatment in regard to the life of men, which on no account one must spread abroad, I will keep to myself, holding such things shameful to be spoken about.

> If I fulfill this oath and do not violate it, may it be granted to me to enjoy life and art, being honored with fame among all men for all time to come; if I transgress it and swear falsely, may the opposite of all this be my lot.

Many states and countries have amended the original oath in favor of an oath that is more "in-line" with "modern" medical ethics. What was seen as a "healing art" is being transformed into a medical "license" to practice however the practitioner or his board sees fit including providing end of life assistance.

Euthanasia, or physician-assisted suicide, is the intentional act of taking a human life to "relieve pain and suffering." Euthanasia can be used by a physician either by withholding treatment that would most probably save life or by administering drugs or other means with the intention to end life. A doctor also may give medicinal means by which their patients can end their own life at home.

No matter how the arguments and reasoning of euthanasia may be humanized or glamorized, these practices are a direct affront to both the sanctity of life and the sovereignty of God. These practices include human beings looking at God and demanding that they have the right to determine what life is worthy of living. 1 Samuel 2:6-8 clearly states on this matter,

> The Lord kills and brings to life; He brings down to Sheol and raises up. The Lord makes poor and makes rich; He brings low and He exalts. He raises up the poor from the dust; He lifts the needy from the ash heap to make them sit with princes and inherit a seat of honor. For the pillars of the earth are the Lord's, and on them He has set the world.

Those who advocate for euthanasia as a "humane" alternative to end of life care argue that it gives three things: autonomy to the patient and doctor to determine their future; management over pain and suffering; and distinction to die at the appointed time and place of the patient's choosing. For centuries a physician intentionally ending the life of a patient was considered anathema, but this sentiment seems to be rapidly changing. Today the marketing ploys behind the movement are crafty as they have labeled euthanasia as "dying with dignity." The God of the Bible teaches the exact opposite, that this doesn't dignify, but actually is an enemy to dignity.

John Bunyan wrote *The Pilgrim's Progress* while in prison in the 1600s. The book was meant to be an allegory of life—what the journey of the Christian looked like through the unfolding tale. While his story is appropriately dark, Bunyan was also almost prophetic in his allegory as to the deceitfulness of evil parading around as light.

In one scene, Christian and Faithful, two characters in the book, enter a city named Vanity Fair. Vanity Fair is a city that seeks to offer to meet every fleshly desire that anyone could dare have. When Christian and Faithful pass through the city without want or desire because of their search for the true joy of the Celestial City, the people are incredulous. The townspeople cannot understand and seek to take these men to their magistrate because they must be "mad" or "imposters." Witnesses bring false accusation against these men, because it cannot be understood how they could not join in the desire of the flesh.

Bunyan describes it this way:

> But the appointed examiners did not believe them, though they did regard them as madmen and lunatics, and likely to be the sort who would bring confusion to the Fair. Therefore, they were detained to be beaten, then besmeared with dirt and caged in such a way as to be made a spectacle to all the men of the Fair. And there they lay for some time while being made the objects of any man's sport or malice or revenge. Meanwhile, the governor of the Fair only continued to laugh at their plight.

This world does not understand dignity. Dignity is not cloaked in man's choice, autonomy, or "right to die." Dignity can only be found in a life that has found joy which cannot be stolen or lost. True dignity cannot be found in autonomy but in surrender to the sovereign control of the Creator who made all life in His image.

Job, a man who suffered greatly but never cursed the Lord, aptly says in Job 1:21, *"Naked I came from my mother's womb, and naked shall I return. The Lord gave, and the Lord has taken away; blessed be the name of the Lord."* Then in Job 14:5, Job says, *"Since his days are determined, and the number of his months is with you, and you have appointed his limits that he cannot pass."* Job understood that although his misery was unbearable, his pain insufferable, and his peace dashed, that the Lord was the one who gave and the Lord was the one who takes away. It is the Lord who is the author of life. We are characters in His grand narrative and we are dependent.

Time Magazine published a story about Charlie and Francie Emerick in March 2018 titled, "This Couple Died By Assisted Suicide Together. Here's Their Story." The story begins, "On the last morning of their lives, Charlie and Francie Emerick held hands. The Portland, Oregon, couple, married for 66 years and both terminally ill, died together in their bed April 20, 2017, after taking lethal doses of medication obtained under the state's Death with Dignity law." Their daughter, Sher Safran, told *Time Magazine*,

> *They had no regrets, no unfinished business. It felt like their time, and it meant so much to know they were together. Their goal was "to help people change the way they think about dying," says Safran, allowing others to share in the mostly private and sometimes clandestine moments leading up to assisted suicide. While it's an increasingly legal and common practice in the U.S., assisted suicide remains mysterious to many.*

The article explains that the couple chronicled their last weeks through video documentary while planning their itinerary for each day leading up to their planned death, even down to the root-beer floats the day before. Their daughter "said she expects strong reactions — including criticism — for chronicling her parents' final days. But she said the documentary honors the Emericks' belief that, if possible, everyone should have a say in when and how they die." Francie Emerick says in the video, "We have a faith that says life is not to be worshipped. It's the quality of life that counts."

Because human beings are created with inherent dignity and created bearing the image of God, determining that our life is not worth living, fundamentally rejects the dignity ascribed by God. God is the one who sovereignly appoints life and death. He tells the ocean where to stop and brings out the starry host one by one and calls them each by name. We must speak out against euthanasia and physician-assisted suicide, because it's a slippery slope into devaluing the intrinsic value of life.

In 2002, Belgium legalized euthanasia, resulting in the death of thousands. Shortly after that, the Netherlands and Luxembourg followed suit. These three countries also highlight a slippery slope. While the Emericks' story from *Time Magazine* is made to sound like a storybook ending, two lovers holding hands while they slip into death, voluntary euthanasia leads to that which is non-voluntary. These three countries are now regularly practicing involuntary euthanasia, which is the killing of sick individuals who are incapable of giving their consent. When we attempt the role of creator and begin to deem certain lives no longer worth living, we begin to see how it affects societies as a whole.

Al Mohler says,

> We decide that life is no longer worth living, but we would rather embrace death. Euthanasia is also broken down between voluntary and involuntary euthanasia. Voluntary euthanasia is what is now classically defined as someone saying, "I want to die. I want you to help me to die." The very fact that the word "euthanasia" is used means there's some kind of intervention by someone. But then you also have the reality of involuntary euthanasia. And this comes down to the fact that a society that embraces euthanasia or physician-assisted suicide is following a logic that says, "At a certain point, this person's life is no longer worth living."
>
> And the logic is easy to extend. "If they are no longer able, if they're incapable of making that determination for themselves, then we will make the determination for them." But it's also very important for us to recognize that economic issues also come into the picture. When people look at the expense of medical care, under certain situations, for certain conditions, over certain amounts of time, for people at certain ages, and they say, "It is no longer really serving a societal benefit to keep this person alive. In order to save money or to allocate precious medical resources, we will simply decide this person's time is up."

In 2019, *The New York Post* published an article, "'Love is letting go:' Netherlands teen raped as child chooses to end her life." The article details the death of Noa Pothoven who decided her life was no longer worth living because of the psychiatric pain she carried from the heinous acts carried out upon her.

Sentiment throughout the Netherlands proclaimed that this was an act of mercy as opposed to murder or suicide. Because the age of consent in the Netherlands is 17, Pothoven was able to decide to die by the assistance of a physician without the consent of her parents. The story reports that Noa had made the request of her parents before her 17th birthday, but they had not agreed. The article reports, "There are no reports of her parents legally challenging her choice at age 17. Although, a year earlier, they refused to give her permission because they thought she should complete trauma treatment, and that her brain should be fully grown before a definitive decision."

The Netherlands continues to add to the terms for legal euthanasia. It seems as though the line between "right and wrong" is fluid and keeps moving, because when we displace God's law for our way, it always leads to a slippery slope and death.

Civilization was created for the protection of people. Medicine was created for healing and health. Neither civilization nor medicine was created to protect "the right to die," but the right to live. Beloved, when we move God off His rightful throne, we should not be surprised when the end is death and insanity. Paul tells the Church of Rome in Romans 13:3-4,

> *Civilization was created for the protection of people. Medicine was created for healing and health. Neither civilization nor medicine was created to protect "the right to die," but the right to live.*

For rulers are not a terror to good conduct, but to bad. Would you have no fear of the one who is in authority? Then do what is good, and you will receive his approval, for he is God's servant for your good. But if you do wrong be afraid for he does not bear the sword in vain. For he is the servant of God, an avenger who carries out God's wrath on the wrongdoer.

Government was created to represent or mirror the protection and authority of God. However, this age has been blinded and has placed personal autonomy and authority on the throne. We throw truth away as rubbish and worship the preferences of man over the order of the Creator.

We may think that being pro-life is simply about defending the rights of a baby to be born. However, we must understand that if we think we have the power and authority to pronounce when life begins, it only follows that we also foolishly believe that we have the authority to determine when life should end. When we lose our pro-life ethic, we lose. Governments meant to be the terror of bad behavior have become a terror to life.

Refugees

Around the world people are fleeing the country of their birth because of famine, poverty, and oppressive governments. In 2015, we saw Egyptian Coptic Christians beheaded on beaches at the hands of their government. We continue to see oppressive regimes in Syria, Iran, and the Middle East approve of the torture, false imprisonment, and killing of their people because of their faith in Christ or because of their outspoken words against the government. In 2018 and 2019, Venezuelans fled from their country en masse into neighboring Colombia because of the tyrants in power over the country.

In Chapter 9 of this book we looked at the life of Ruth who was an immigrant and refugee who ended up in the fields of Boaz. Ruth's father-in-law was a Jew and he left Israel because of a severe famine. He was a refugee in the land of Moab and then in turn after his and his sons' deaths, Ruth the Moabitess becomes a refugee in the land of Israel. It cannot be emphasized enough that Moab and Israel were fierce enemies, much in the same way as the nations of India and Pakistan in the 21st century. People of the same heritage, but very disparate views and lives.

The question at hand is how do we think biblically about refugees, especially in light of the promise of the 2016 election to build a wall between the U.S. and Mexico and then have Mexico pay for it? How do we obey Scripture as God's chosen people and love the stranger and alien, while also understanding that open borders are the antithesis of sovereign nations?

As we look around the world, I think there are two very distinct issues surrounding refugees. And these issues need the response of two very different groups of people. I have had the amazing opportunity to travel to over 40 sovereign nations. Whenever I leave the U.S., I must take my passport with me. In many of the countries that I visit frequently, I am also required to gain permission for my visit from their appropriate authorities for which I am granted a visa for entry. No matter how I enter into these sovereign nations, I am granted a window of time that I may legally stay within the borders of each nation. Some of these time periods are as short as the total duration of my quick trip, or ranging up to 365 days. I need permission to dwell within the borders of these nations.

The first issue, therefore, of the refugee crisis is the civil protection of the citizens for each nation of the world. These civil protections range and are varied depending on the needs of the nations around the world. For the U.S., most of the international terrorist attacks committed on American soil were by men who infiltrated one of the many land borders of the U.S. So the responsibility for the civil protection of the U.S. includes national security. This, however, also extends to the provision of government services offered to the tax paying citizens of the U.S. Our civil services thrive on visitors from other nations, but they survive by the appropriate tax revenue of those who are here legally and working within legal confines. Civil protection for U.S. citizens through the provision of immigration services can only be financed through representative taxation.

I have been privileged to spend much time in the country of Colombia, especially over the last several years. In the summer of 2018 my family and I had the opportunity to spend five weeks serving in four cities throughout Colombia. I have seen first hand the poverty of Colombia and the effects of

Venezuelans migrating en masse into the country. Colombians are a gracious and accommodating people who have been helped immensely by other nations during their own crises; however, in Colombia, the resources and support of the government is already lacking for current citizenship. The Colombian government has many needs for her people that the international community has helped bring to bear. An influx of refugees from Venezuela strains an already struggling infrastructure. Therefore, Colombia's immigration program is a civil protection for the survival of her citizens.

Yet another issue surrounding the refugee crisis around the world is inhumane injustice and oppression. This oppression comes either through acts of commission or omission. Some nations neglect their people, abuse the poor, and enslave the needy. People flee from their country of origin in order to live, survive and hopefully thrive. Also, there are tyrannical governments such as those in many Middle Eastern countries, North Korea, Southeast Asian nations, Venezuela and others who oppress their dissidents, murder Christians, and suppress the God-given freedoms given to men. People flee these nations to save their lives and to escape injustice.

How in the world do we rectify these two very real and competing issues? If only it were simple. This is such an incredibly complex issue.

I believe that biblically we must look at the life of Daniel and Esther to see that the responses to each of these issues must be addressed by two distinct groups. The first group, government; the second, the people of God.

First, in both of these biblical accounts we see that Daniel and Esther are living in exile in Babylon as refugees. While neither Esther nor Daniel had fled from Israel to Babylon, they had been forcibly exiled — a situation very similar to that of a refugee. Esther must speak out for the injustice of her people at the hand of evil Haman who had convinced King Xerxes to commit genocide among the entire Jewish remnant. King Xerxes enforced this because of people's unwillingness to bow to the authority of an earthly king over their loyalty to their Heavenly King.

While Esther goes before the king in a move of bold and reckless abandon, her plea is one of justice for her people by showing the faithful service her uncle, Mordecai, a Jew, had given to the king. Esther speaks up for justice and serves her exiled people, who are living as refugees in a strange land, but never judges the king's immigration policy. Esther knows that the king is not a follower of God, but that he is the ruler of a sovereign nation. She is called to influence, speak out, and minister to the refugee, but not to amend the ways of an entire nation.

The truth is that Babylon was not Israel and neither is the U.S. or many other nations. Israel isn't just a nation, but is a people united and chosen by God. The Lord gives national decrees to Israel to care for the alien, stranger and refugee that aren't meant to be for governments, but for His people.

In Daniel, we see a similar setting and response. Daniel lived during the reign of several ruthless kings of Babylon. These kings were prideful, narcissistic, and would have abused Twitter had it been invented. Daniel lived and postured his life in such a way that he was highly esteemed by all of these kings. Because he was wise, honest, integrous, and smart, he earned a high standing among a pagan government. Daniel refused to alter his devotion to God in order to satisfy his standing in the kingdom.

Daniel was faithful to God and knew that his position in the kingdom was one of favor and protection of God's chosen people. King Darius, who dearly loved Daniel, is tricked by his advisors to throw every person praying to anyone but the king into a den of lions. Daniel knows the edict, and he knows he cannot comply. Instead of pleading at the feet of the king, insisting on policy changes, Daniel is faithful in his love for Israel's true King and continues living a life devoted to God.

King Darius's advisors, who are waiting in anticipation, pounce on Daniel and take him to the king. The king realizes what has been done and must throw Daniel unjustly into the hungry lion's den. Even as Darius exacts the unfair verdict upon loyal Daniel, he prays for the salvation of Daniel. The next morning, the lions are calm and Daniel is cuddled up next to them because God had indeed spared Daniel.

Beloved, there is no question that God's people are to visit the refugee, to speak out for justice, and even do their best to influence the policy of governments when they are unjust and unfair toward the alien. There is also no question that governments, while representative of God, are not a substitute for the Church. Governments are pagan and secular.

Throughout the Bible, we see in both the Old and New Testaments evil kings, imperfect governors, and ruthless caesars. In response, we see the Church living out authentic lives counter-cultural to these leaders in such a way that the gospel of King Jesus is proclaimed with boldness.

So Church, we must know that government has its place in imperfectly trying to solve immigration issues and refugee crises; however, their role was meant to be incomplete so that the Church — the image bearers of almighty God — might be able to show the justice of God to those in need.

We must visit and care for refugees from the Middle East displaced in Turkey and throughout Europe while speaking out for justice and aid to governments and leaders. We must care for innocent children who many times are the collateral damage to either their parents' poor decisions or their parents' desperation. And we must visit and care for the refugees who are locked in detention centers along the U.S. border with Mexico, all while advocating for their care and support.

Our God calls us to visit and to care for the hurting without prejudice. God's Word tells us to go without condemnation and show the grace of Christ. Think about it this way: when a parent sees their children bleeding, hurting, or injured they do not go to their child and ask first, "How did this happen and how did you get into this shape?" Let's say the child was being foolish, careless, or started a fight — we wouldn't withhold care, concern, and aid. As a matter of fact, a good parent rushes to the aid of their child without considering the guilt or innocence of the child.

However, I feel that when it comes to caring for refugees, as a Church we first want to examine the culpability of that refugee. We want them exonerated before we reach out. Beloved, this is neither biblical nor pro-life. I thank the Lord that Chuck Colson, founder of Prison Fellowship, began to show love, care, and aid to prisoners no matter their guilt, because it is through this ministry that so many have been freed from the bondage of sin, guilt, and shame.

When it comes to the immigration policies of nations around the world, we can be neither surprised nor shocked when governments act according to their own understood best interests. We speak up and influence policy when and where we can, but we also live knowing that ultimately these nations that hold our passports are not our true home.

Pilgrims and Aliens

Ultimately, we care for the refugees and the vulnerable because that's exactly who we are until our lives and wills are surrendered to the Lordship of Christ. Jesus came to transform orphans into children of God, refugees into citizens of the Kingdom, and the vulnerable into the saints who follow the King.

And this is why we, as image bearers of the Most High God, must be pro-life and not just pro-birth. Our pro-life ethic shows the justice of the kingdom for the marginalized, the trafficked, the LGBTQ+, the woman, the fatherless, the widow, the orphan, and the person living with special needs. Our gospel-driven justice shows the power and hope of the gospel.

I know that so many complex issues have been discussed in these pages. Many of these topics and realities could cause us to despair or lose hope. Instead the hope is that we would be boldly called to do justice, to love mercy, and to walk humbly with our God. The aim is not the loss of hope in this world, but a greater and higher hope in the King who will one day redeem all of the brokenness.

This world is like looking at your reflection in a broken or shattered mirror. We see not perfection, but the flaws; however, if we look closely enough we can see beautiful glimpses of what God created this world to be.

Each year my family and I have been blessed by dear friends and partners in ministry to use their beach house in early fall. These trips are such a rich blessing and have been times of true and deep refreshment. We look forward with anticipation to beach week each year.

However, each beach week has had its own funny troubles or imperfections. One such week an escaped convict was hiding out in the small community and was apprehended after a 48-hour manhunt about 100 yards from where we were sleeping. Christopher Stringer became a Newell household name as our children's papers were penned for school and his name lived in beach lore infamy.

Then there were the years of the sand worms (little needles in the ocean), the red tide, the sand lice, biting flies, and the overpopulation of seaweed. Even though we look out to the ocean and the beauty of these weeks, we realize they aren't perfect weeks, but simply a sliver of the glory of God as we stare at the ocean, enjoy the pastels of the setting sun, and bask in the salty ocean breeze. Creation is marred and, beloved, if you are a Christ-follower, then this is not your home. You are an exile and pilgrim.

The Apostle Peter says it this way in 1 Peter 2:11-12: *"Beloved, I urge you as sojourners and exiles to abstain from the passions of the flesh, which wage war against your soul. Keep your conduct among the Gentiles honorable, so that when they speak against you as evildoers, they may see your good deeds and glorify God on the day of visitation."*

A marred creation and a sin-sick world should not surprise or shock us. Sinners sin and lost people act lost. And such were we before we were washed by the blood of Christ. So pilgrim and refugee looking forward to the coming Kingdom, take heart and take action.

We of all people know of the coming Kingdom and must speak out for life created in the image of God. We must demonstrate gospel-driven justice for the orphan, widow, poor, vulnerable, and stranger. When we speak up and reach out in the love of Christ we are putting a taste of the coming Kingdom onto the lips of those around us.

It's like the Japanese Hibachi restaurant at the food court of every local mall. They stand out in the corridor giving out samples of teriyaki and bourbon chicken, not so that the taste will satisfy, but that the sample will leave you craving for more.

If we live lives of radical obedience, we will be ignored by some, hated by others, and mocked just like the poor guy hawking the chicken at the mall. However, to those who take notice and sample the glory of God, Lord willing, they will develop a thirst for which only the grace of God will satisfy.

This is not our home, so instead of blending in with this world, let's live in such a way as to demonstrate that we are aliens and visitors who are longing for our true home. A home where the image bearers of God live in the presence of the true King.

> And I saw no temple in the city, for its temple is the Lord God the Almighty and the Lamb. And the city has no need of sun or moon to shine on it, for the glory of God gives it light, and its lamp is the Lamb. By its light will the nations walk, and the kings of the earth will bring their glory into it, and its gates will never be shut by day — and there will be no night there. They will bring into it the glory and the honor of the nations. But nothing unclean will ever enter it, nor anyone who does what is detestable or false, but only those who are written in the Lamb's book of life. —**Revelation 21:22-27**

Discussion Questions

1. Reflecting on Acts 4:32-35, contrast scripture's view of family with the world's view. Do you see any contrast between this scripture and your own family of faith?

2. How can Acts 4:32-35 apply specifically to caring for the elderly? How can you care for the older members in your congregation or support those caring for the aging in their own families?

3. How are euthanasia and physician-assisted suicide slippery slopes into devaluing the intrinsic value of life?

4. How do the Biblical accounts of Esther and Daniel change or inform your desire to care for image bearing refugees?

5. How are you living in a way that demonstrates a longing for our true home? How are you inviting all image bearers to share in that coming Kingdom with you?

APPENDIX

Becoming a Godly Man

Excerpt from *"5 Characteristics of a Godly Man"* by Todd Wagner,
pastor of Watermark Community Church in Dallas, Texas

1. **Step Up. Lead. Initiate. Be a man of action. Assume it is your job and your moment. Hate apathy. Reject passivity.**

   (2 Samuel 10:7; 10:12; Ezekiel 22:30; Psalm 101; Proverbs 14:23; Proverbs 20:6; Jeremiah 5:1; Ezekiel 22:23-31; John 10:11-13; James 1:23-25)

2. **Speak Out: Silence in the midst of sin is a sin. Be courageous. Fear God, not man. Speak the truth in love.**

   (Proverbs 27:5-6; Proverbs 31:8-9; 1 Peter 3:15; Proverbs 14:25; Proverbs 15:1-2; Proverbs 24:11-12; Isaiah 8:11-13; Jeremiah 1:17; Romans 1:16)

3. **Stand Strong: Don't give in when you are challenged, attacked, or criticized.**

   (Jeremiah 1:18-19; 1 Corinthians 15:58; 1 Peter 5:8-9; 2 Chronicles 16:9; Proverbs 24:10; Isaiah 41:10; Jeremiah 12:5; 1 Corinthians 10:13; Galatians 1:10; Philippians 1:27-28)

4. **Stay Humble: Be vigilant against pride. Get the log out of your eye. Don't think less of yourself; think of yourself less.**

   (Psalm 141:5; 1 Peter 5:5-7; Proverbs 3:5-6; Proverbs 12:1; Isaiah 66:2; Micah 6:8; John 15:5; Philippians 2:3-5)

5. **Serve the King. Seek first His Kingdom, His glory, and His righteousness. Hope in the eternal. Live for a greater reward.**

   (Matthew 6:33; Mark 10:45; Joshua 24:14-15; Psalm 16:11; Psalm 84:10-12; 2 Corinthians 5:10; Hebrews 6:10; 1 Peter 2:21-23)

Becoming a Godly Woman

Five thoughts on Godly Women (Todd Wagner, Lead Pastor of Watermark Community Church in Dallas, Texas gives Five Impactful ways for women to honor the Lord with their lives.

1. **Seek God first. Reject the lie that anything or anyone else can satisfy you.**

   (Matthew 6:33-34, 1 Chronicles 16:8-12, Psalm 9:10, Psalm 27:1-5, Psalm 34: 10-14, Psalm 40:16, Jeremiah 29:11-13, Zephaniah 2:3, Matthew 6:25-34)

2. **Speak Faithfully. Love others with godly wisdom, boldness, and kindness as a faithful completer of others.**

   (Genesis 2:18, Proverbs 27:5-6, Proverbs 31:8-9, Proverbs 31:26, Psalm 19:14, Proverbs 12:18, Proverbs 13:3, Proverbs 16:13, Proverbs 20:15, Proverbs 24:26)

3. **Show true Beauty. Bodies deteriorate; persons develop. Invest in that which lasts.**

   (Proverbs 31:30, 1 Timothy 2:9-10, 1 Samuel 16:7, Proverbs 11:22, 1 Peter 3:3-5)

4. **Stay Humble: Be constantly aware of pride and selfishness. Don't think less of yourself but think of yourself less.**

   (Isaiah 66:2, Philippians 2:3-5, Psalm 141:5, Proverbs 3:5-6, Proverbs 12:1, Micah 6:8, John 15:5, 1 Peter 3:8-9,1 Peter 5:5-7)

5. **Serve the Lord: Set your mind on eternal things, serve the eternal King, and live to please only Him.**

   (John 12:25-26, Galatians 1:10, Colossians 3:23, Psalm 16:11, Psalm 84:10-12, Mark 10:42-45, 2 Corinthians 5:10, Philippians 1:21, Hebrews 6:10, 1 Peter 2:21-23)

Book Suggestions for Families

Hero Tales: A Family Treasury of True Stories from the Lives of Christian Heroes by Dave and Neta Jackson

Christian Heroes Then and Now Series by Janet and George Benge

Window on the World: An Operation World Prayer Resource

The Jesus Storybook Bible by Sally Lloyd Jones

Thoughts to Make Your Heart Sing by Sally Lloyd Jones

13 Ways to Ruin Your Life: A Practical Guide for Guys by Jarrod Jones

God's Names by Sally Michael

On This Day in Christian History by Robert J. Morgan

Then Sings My Soul by Robert J. Morgan

Made in the USA
Columbia, SC
20 November 2020